The Flywheel of Life and Leadership

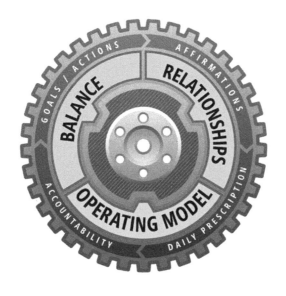

ED RAPP
WITH ANJU JAIN

PAGE PUBLISHING
Conneaut Lake, PA

First originally published by Page Publishing 2022

All proceeds from sales of *The Flywheel of Life and Leadership* will be donated to Answer ALS (answerals.org).

ISBN 978-1-6624-6631-1 (pbk)
ISBN 979-8-88654-028-4 (hc)
ISBN 978-1-6624-6632-8 (digital)

Printed in the United States of America

Contents

Acknowledgments

I used this photo countless times during my days at Caterpillar to illustrate a critical point that applies to this book. I am growing into the shoes of what it takes to be a good human being and a good leader. I do not profess to have all the answers. This book simply captures where I am in my personal journey.

I want to thank the "review committee" for their unfiltered feedback and guidance and Jenn for her creative support. You will see references to authors who influenced my perspective and leaders who molded me. I have been guided and shaped by so many.

The creation of this book was a true team effort in collaboration with Anju. While the framework was built on my background and experiences, Anju's research and experience as a writer is what helped make it all possible. For me, she is not only a coauthor but also a dear friend.

Lastly and most importantly, a thank-you to my wife, Ann; our children Jay, Ali, and Stef and their spouses; and "Da Boys"—our four grandsons—Cole, Eli, Leo, and Brody. When I was diagnosed with ALS, my doctor said, "This is a tough disease. You will need a strong support network." I told him, "We have that one covered."

Foreword

We often ask ourselves if it is truly possible to have it all. Can I be a successful parent, spouse, leader, employee, and friend and be happy while doing it? This book helps explore exactly that and come away with proven lessons that work. I'm currently a leader with Caterpillar and had the pleasure of working in Ed Rapp's organizations for large portions of my 30 year career. I was blessed to have Ed as a mentor, sponsor, and friend throughout my career. Today, I still live by many life and leadership lessons he instilled in me. Because of Ed's teachings, I have risen through the ranks and also found time to have a successful marriage and raise two wonderful daughters. Ed's approach and lessons have helped me have a rewarding life and career.

Ed has been gone from Caterpillar for more than six years now. But he is still one of the most popular speakers for leadership engagements and inspirational discussions inside and outside Caterpillar. His lessons on balance, relationships, and having an effective operating model along with his amazingly disciplined approach permeated our company and continue to inspire audiences. Not many weeks go by without me hearing someone quoting from his leadership lessons. Ed not only believes in these concepts but also lives them every day. His exceptional success at Caterpillar, and now with Answer ALS, is a testament to how these elements lead to breakthrough results, foster amazing relationships, and make a positive impact on others. Ed once sat at my kitchen table when I was contemplating returning to work after my second child. He helped me see I could come back if I created a vision, set the parameters of what was important to me, and planned my personal life with the same rigor as my work life. I did come back, part-time at first, but then full-time later. Ed's lessons create success not only for him but also for those around him.

Balance, relationships, and a clear operating model are at the heart of his leadership and this book. Striking a balance is one of the toughest concepts, but the book provides excellent ideas on how to make that happen, using discipline and setting priorities. I remember him calling me out of the blue one day to ask if I had time for lunch. He told me to bring my teammates. Even as an Executive Office member, Ed took the time to get to know people at all levels of our company. He invited employees to impromptu lunches, worked alongside them, and made the extra effort to help people find career and personal success. These relationships serve as multipliers in creating breakthrough success.

The book also discusses the need for a clear operating model and definition of winning. These elements are at the heart of any winning team. I remember working with Ed when we started the new operating model to improve one part of our business. He led his team to define success clearly and then identified expectations of how we should run the business to get there. He didn't just give us a presentation and leave. He first created a document that we could reference, and then consistently checked in, assuring we all understood, and made sure we celebrated success. That rigor allowed us to run our portion of the business every day, delivering our piece of the overall plan. When a team has clarity on the definition of winning and knows how they need to work, the power of the flywheel can be harnessed. The result is you get acceleration and results. This book shows true success stories using this model.

When Ed left Caterpillar after sharing his Amyotrophic Lateral Sclerosis (ALS) diagnosis, we wondered what would happen to this bright light and exceptional leader. Yet, it didn't take long to see another shining example of this man's principles come to life. Most of us would have seen Ed's diagnosis as an impossible obstacle. But he shows us that with balance, relationships, leveraging an operating model, and approaching life with rigor, positive energy, and discipline, you can hit the most difficult curveballs out of the park. I can't think of a better person to write a book on life and leadership because Ed has proven this works around the world, and in multiple industries and scenarios. The topic of life and leadership is huge. This story is about bringing together simple but effective elements with a disciplined approach. It's a recipe to become a brilliant leader and have a successful and fulfilling life.

I can assure you, the model espoused in this book has stood the test of time. Thousands of employees I have worked with, can vouch for its effectiveness. We all carry so much of it with us every day. Thank you to Ed for shining his light on all of us and for sharing insights with everyone who reads this book.

Kristin Girard
Vice President of Distribution
Caterpillar Inc.

* * *

In early March 2018, about a dozen people sat around a table at a restaurant in downtown Baltimore. They were neurologists and neuroscientists from top-tier institutes, business executives from Fortune 100 companies, experts in machine learning and artificial intelligence—all hardworking, top-of-their-game, successful individuals. As we waited for our entrées to arrive, the discussion turned to the intensity of the week. It was Thursday evening, and for the past four days, we'd been together in a hotel conference room, reviewing data and plans for our shared endeavor—Answer ALS. For two hundred years, researchers have been trying to crack the nut that is ALS, a devasting neurological disease. We had come together to do things differently, to apply our collective knowledge, formulate and execute a plan that we all hoped would be the beginning of the end for ALS. I was feeling content with how the week had passed and the progress we had made, but I was also spent. Most of us know how these types of meetings and conferences go—you're "on" all the time.

Since we were on the subject, I ventured a comment about the importance of striking a work-life balance. I don't remember my exact words, but it was something along the lines of, "I think it's important to balance a week like this with some recovery time—a couple of days to totally unplug and reset." I looked up and saw some surprised faces. But there was one person who met my gaze and nodded in agreement—Ed Rapp. He took my point, which for a moment I thought might have sunk the conversation along with my colleague's view of me as a hard worker, and added to it: "I think that's right, Emily. You come back stronger and more focused." Coming from someone like Ed, that comment carried weight.

When I heard he planned to write a book on the subject, I was thrilled. Working with Ed over the past number of years, I recognize how learning his method and philosophy has been hugely helpful, not just to the Answer ALS program, but also to me personally. I'm a neuroscientist at Johns Hopkins, a wife, and a mother to two beautiful, rambunctious boys. My husband is a physician with his own practice. Life is full. Like many of us, I often wonder, Am I doing this right? Am I meeting my family's needs? Am I crushing it at work? In *The Flywheel of Life and Leadership*, Ed provides guidance for being the best you, in the workplace and at home. The book is a collection of commonsense advice and strategies that can greatly impact your ability to get things done and embrace life. Relating through examples from his own life and experiences, Ed shares the attributes and methods that led him to become an admired leader, first at Caterpillar and then at Answer ALS.

In a wonderful analogy that emanates from his career with the construction and engineering giant, he conveys core concepts of the book as elements of a flywheel—a mechanical device designed to increase a machine's momentum, provide greater stability, and give a smooth release of power, qualities as essential to any leader as they are to a machine.

The leadership flywheel embraces three principles: balance, relationships, and operating model. For each, Ed walks us through the core concepts so we had a firm understanding of the required components. This often requires the reader to take time to think through their own situation, putting pen to paper to clearly define their goals and priorities. Ed asks, "What is your definition of winning?" In other words, what gives your life meaning? He argues that a clearly defined vision inspires focus and commitment, simplifies our decisions, and increases the potential for success in all aspects of life.

Not by chance, balance and relationships are covered first. The journey to effective leadership starts with self. Are we in balance mentally and physically? Are we building and maintaining relationships that are most important to us? Ed underscores the necessity of planning your personal and professional life with equal rigor and provides tips on managing both. Our availability for significant work or personal events should not be left to chance. He states, "Efficiency will set you free," and I couldn't agree more. We all know the feeling of returning home on the heels of a productive day. It's so much easier to be truly present and engage with family or friends. Wouldn't it be nice to have more days like that? Applying the strategies laid out in this book, Ed provides a path to that possibility. "It's not about less work; it's about doing the work you do more efficiently."

In today's world, that means managing a near-constant stream of emails and meeting requests. Hopping from one Zoom meeting to the next and trying to do "the real work" in between. Ed provides guidance on how to keep technology working for us so that we remain productive and proactive and don't fall into the trap of simply keeping up.

When he joined the Answer ALS team as chair of the advisory board, Ed brought a distinct approach and operating model—and we are better for it. His first question was, "What's the definition of winning here?" Wasn't it obvious? Cure ALS! But what Ed was really asking for was a shared and specific definition of success. Answer ALS is a consortium of clinics and research institutes spread across the U.S. Did all 120-plus members know and share a single vision? We quickly got to work drafting a mission statement. While presentations and conversations can be interpreted in many ways, Ed taught us that a clear written mission statement serves as powerful foundation for any organization.

Our mission is to build the most comprehensive clinical and biological assessment of ALS in history, leading to the discovery of disease subtypes, so that researchers and scientists across the globe are equipped to understand and ultimately end ALS.

Once we established our goals, it was time to craft an operating model to evaluate and monitor our progress. Working with the head researcher for each arm of the program, we identified the target milestones and monthly metrics to keep the program on track and within budget. While such an approach might be second nature in many sectors, I will tell you it's not always the case in academic research. We were bringing best practices in business together with academic excellence and scaling it to industry levels. As I mentioned, Answer ALS is a paradigm shift in neurodegenerative disease research. Our experiments are typically conducted on fewer than a dozen samples at a time. Answer ALS set an ambitious goal to work with samples derived from over one thousand ALS and healthy control participants. To achieve that, we had to identify research labs that were best in class in terms of science and could also scale to process and analyze the required number of samples.

Operationally, we were integrating efforts and funding across 24 organizations. Ed helped us create a meeting structure and cadence that ensured all partners had a voice and could remain in alignment as the effort progressed. That's especially important for a long-term project like Answer ALS. The team has been working together for over six years now and often hear people remark that you'd never guess the group is comprised of individuals from so many different institutes. When we're together, first and foremost, we work as members of Answer ALS. I believe that's a reflection of our leadership, particularly, Ed. In *The Flywheel of Life and Leadership*, he highlights the importance of getting to know your team. In his mind, keeping the channels of communication and trust open at all levels of the organization is a key aspect of effective leadership. Ed fosters an environment of transparency and respect that inspires us all to do our best work.

The concepts laid out by Ed in *The Flywheel of Life and Leadership* go a long way to help the reader determine life goals and set a plan to achieve them. As he does in person, Ed will continue, through this book, to bring out the best in us as leaders and as humans.

Emily Baxi, PhD Director, Milken Institute
Center for Strategic Philantrophy
Former Executive Director of the Packard
Center at Johns Hopkins

Introduction

Piracicaba, Brazil

At some point in life, we are faced with tough questions for which there are no easy answers. For me, this happened on November 5, 2015, when I had to respond to questions like these:

1. How do you go from working 37 years with one company, taking only two sick days and then being told you have 2–5 years to live?

2. How do you go everywhere your employer asks you to go, do everything they ask you to do, and then walk away twelve months before potentially becoming the CEO of a great company?

These were just a couple of questions that came to mind following my ALS diagnosis on that cold and rainy November day at the Mayo Clinic. ALS, is a progressive, fatal, neurodegenerative illness that attacks motor neurons. When motor neurons die, the ability of the brain to control muscle movement is lost, leading to paralysis. Unable to function, muscles atrophy. Eventually, all muscles under voluntary control are affected, in time, patients lose the ability to walk, talk, swallow, and breathe. During this horrible process, the mind remains completely intact, observing the loss of each function. When the diaphragm and chest muscles fail, patients stop breathing on their own. Sadly enough, there is neither a known cause of the disease nor a cure.

Dealing with my challenge has helped me understand that, at some point in time, everyone deals with adversity in life. It could be loss of a job, the loss of a loved one, a diagnosis, or as the entire world experienced, a pandemic that turned our lives upside down. It is important to realize that we will not be measured by an event or single occurrence, but by how we respond to such harsh realities. The time to start preparing for that eventual curveball in life is not when it is leaving the pitcher's hand. Instead, preparation is in how one lives and leads along the way, every day, long before adversity strikes.

The possibility of putting my thoughts down in writing was planted back in 2006 on a trip to Brazil. Our Caterpillar factory in Piracicaba, Brazil, has a great tradition of planting a tree in honor of visiting company officers. During that tree-planting ceremony, the gardener turned to me and said something in Portuguese, which I, of course, did not understand. So, I asked for a translation.

The facility's general manager translated, "Every person has three responsibilities in life. The first is to have kids to create the next generation. The second is to plant a tree to protect the environment for the next generation. And the third is to write a book to pass on knowledge to the next generation."

This conversation remained in the back of my mind—that while I had now fulfilled two of the three responsibilities, perhaps I needed to complete the journey of writing a book as well.

The final nudge to put my thoughts down in writing came from recognizing that the life and leadership principles that worked well during my career at Caterpillar also translated into the world of my ALS work and beyond. While I made the tough decision to retire from Caterpillar, I remain active, including being part of Answer ALS—the largest and most comprehensive ALS research project in history. My time and roles in both corporate and research environments have led me to believe that the principles I leveraged to lead my life and a large business portfolio at Caterpillar are equally relevant in my current role as the board chair of Answer ALS.

This is a book on life and leadership. I am a visual learner, so the concepts are presented as a simple framework, one that I believe is relevant both at home and work, in all kinds of situations and challenges. It does not matter what industry you are in or what role you play. Yes, many of the examples are Caterpillar-related. That is what happens when you stay at one company for your entire career. While your situation is undoubtedly different, I firmly believe this framework will effectively translate to your circumstances and challenges.

Having worked at an engineering company, it is no surprise that my concepts of the leadership framework are built around a flywheel, a critical component between the engine and transmission. Flywheels are typically found in internal combustion engines and have been used for decades to power machines. They smooth out the output torque pulses caused by the periodic firing of cylinders. Energy is stored very briefly, for less than one revolution of the flywheel and then the energy is transferred to other machine components.

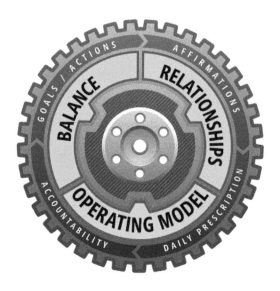

Just as a flywheel transfers power from a motor to a machine, we, as leaders, transfer power to other people through how we live and lead. The inherent principles need to move in sync to do our job as leaders. The principles include:

- *Balance.* This flywheel principle focuses on planning your personal life with the same rigor and discipline as your professional life. As in a machine application, the flywheel must be in balance. You need the right mass in the right place, enabling it to turn at a high velocity. If it goes out of balance, it wastes energy in vibrations and the forces created do not transfer the required power to the rest of the machine, thereby compromising its efficiency.

   The same applies to each of us: If we lack balance in our lives, it directly affects the energy we transfer as we live and lead. The pursuit of a professional career at the expense of everything and everyone else can lead to a shallow victory. I acknowledge that life is rarely in perfect balance. Picture a teeter-totter—you are constantly working to find the balance point. The key is to be consciously aware of your state and work toward bringing it into balance.

Critical pieces of planning your personal life involve making a plan, introducing efficiencies in the way you work, and becoming a "corporate athlete," which is about taking care of your physical, emotional, and mental well-being.

- *Relationships.* The second principle of the flywheel is about investing in your relationships. Similar to a machine flywheel where the bulk of the weight is carried on the edges to maximize power generation, so is the case for effective leadership. When you put too much mass or emphasis in the center (or at the top in a typical hierarchical organizational chart), you fail to leverage your entire organization, which leads to inertia and suboptimal outcomes.

   Instead, your ability to lead and inspire depends on building relationships throughout the organization and demonstrating genuine care about your people. This is all the more important, because the higher you move up the organization, the greater the number of filters between you and the truth. To overcome these barriers and deliver results, you need to build relationships by showing you care, unpacking your bags, getting your hands dirty, and integrating this activity in your calendar tool.

- *Operating Model.* A flywheel only works when it is built according to an engineering drawing or blueprint. Your business needs a similar structure leading to clarity of direction.

   To drive value as a leader, you need a disciplined approach that provides your entire organization/team with an unequivocal clear direction, grounded with an understanding of the external environment and a clear definition of winning. You must focus on the few things that make the biggest difference, a governance structure that permeates the entire organization, and a cadence that creates pace.

These three principles—balance, relationships and operating model—are critical to being an effective leader. It is important to recognize that they do not function in isolation but rather each constantly interacts with the other to keep the flywheel (be it in a machine or in leadership) in constant motion.

Depending on your current situation, implementing these concepts may require changes in how you live and lead. That can be a difficult task because the mind attempts to regulate our habits and revert us to a state of familiarity based on our past practices and behaviors. Just as a flywheel needs oil for lubrication to help all the moving parts run smoothly, we all need to develop habits to ensure we run smoothly as well.

Change will only happen when you deploy a process of "discipline leading to habits" that includes intentional goal setting and action planning supported by affirmations, a daily prescription, and tracking your performance over time to drive accountability.

While there are numerous books on leadership that cover these individual components, I believe in the benefits of integrating them together under one framework. The concepts are supported by research and grounded in real-life situations I experienced on my journey from a farm boy in Missouri to becoming a group president at Caterpillar, and leading an effort to unravel the mysteries of ALS. These principles have stood the test of time through the many highs and lows of my life. Although the experiences outlined are very personal, I am confident they will be relevant to you, regardless of where you are in your life.

The book is for those who want to up their game and enrich their personal and professional lives. It is for those who are not only aspiring to climb the corporate ladder and lead people but are also thinking about their personal goals and well-being. This discussion is not about achieving one at the expense of the other but rather how to excel at both personal and work lives. Finally, it is also for those who want to get a head start in preparing for the eventual curveballs one may encounter in life.

As you read this book, understand that many of the concepts presented are simply good old common sense. My intent is not to state the obvious; it is to raise awareness and push you to assess and achieve a life you want. Some additional thoughts to keep in mind:

INTRODUCTION

1. There are several ways to get to a destination. The flywheel is not an explicit prescription but a framework you can approach in your own way. I encourage you to use these ideas as a starting point to build your own method. I am confident the concepts will serve as thought provokers to prepare you for your life's journey.

2. There are no silver bullets. Living and leading a designed life is hard, but is absolutely worth the effort.

3. It is not about doing less work; it is about making choices to be more effective and efficient at the work you do.

4. Life will not always be in balance or the way you want it, and that is perfectly okay too. You simply need to be consciously aware when it is not and then do your best to swing it back into balance.

5. Finally, it is all a matter of choice. As Victor Frankl, in his book *Man's Search for Meaning*,[1] said, "Choice, is the last of the human freedoms." Only you can choose what you do with the concepts and principles. I suggest that you choose wisely.

Let me close the introduction with two critical disclaimers. First, while I firmly believe in the principles outlined in this book, I am still on the journey of what it takes to be a good leader and a good human being. In fact, we all are. When it comes to life or leadership, it is naive to think any of us has "arrived." It is an endless journey. Secondly, you can live and lead without focusing on all three principles of the flywheel. There are leaders who do not have balance in their lives or relationships at all levels of an organization or who do not execute an explicit operating model. I believe this approach yields suboptimal results, but it gets down to your own personal definition of success. This should be an explicit choice on your part.

To get you started on your journey, I recommend you complete an assessment of where you stand today. Take the time to make notes on the self-assessment in Appendix 1, page 122.

Getting to Know Me

Early childhood home, Pilot Grove, Missouri

One of my mentors was the former Chairman and CEO of Caterpillar, Jim Owens. He believed that a big part of leadership is storytelling, so let me begin with my story.

I hail from the small town of Pilot Grove, Missouri, population just over seven hundred. I am the middle child of seven, with three older brothers and three younger sisters. I used to complain to my mom, "I am the neglected middle child."

Her response was always the same: "With seven kids, you're all neglected. Get over it."

While in my early days it was seven children in a two-bedroom, one-bathroom house (pictured above), the reality was, there was no neglect and I grew up in a family where I was surrounded by love, faith, and great experiences.

Given that we all are products of our environment, the concepts outlined in this book are heavily influenced by my childhood experiences. They are also influenced by my willingness to take a chance. Of the seven children in my family, I was the first to go to a four-year university, even though my high school counselor doubted my capability. He felt I was much more suited for a small college than a major university. For some reason, I wanted more. After graduating in a class of 30 from Pilot Grove High School in 1975, I headed 36 miles down the road to the University of Missouri (Mizzou).

My initial plan was to become a high school basketball coach. I loved all sports, particularly basketball, and felt that I could have a positive impact on young people. However, for some strange reason, one of my professors decided to head me down a different path. After I finished his course in the second semester of my freshman year, he pulled me aside and said, "Listen, if you want to coach kids, you can always do it as a volunteer. You should broaden your mind and consider other possibilities, as you have some hidden talents that need to be fully realized." This started a trend of others believing in me more than I did myself. His coaching eventually led me to change my major to finance. It was not the function of some personality survey trying to find the right major; it just felt like the right direction for me.

While at Mizzou, I always sensed that I was working against the odds. I remember, during my freshman year, walking around the campus with a few friends I had met from the "big cities" of St. Louis and Kansas City. They were talking about Advanced Placement (AP) courses and how they were already second-semester freshmen. I asked them, "Where do you sign up for these AP courses?" to which they laughed and responded, "Back in high school." Pilot Grove did not offer courses that allowed high school students to earn college credits, so I knew from the beginning that the odds were stacked against me. While I might not have been the smartest young man on campus, I did know how to work hard. This sense of working hard to overcome some of the shortcomings of my background was a chip that remained on my shoulder for a number of years, helping propel me through four years at Mizzou, where I graduated with honors.

Although I had a finance degree when I set about looking for a job after graduating from college, I was not interested in the banking sector. I was more intrigued by business. When I interviewed with companies that came on campus, I did what every college kid does and researched the company, the products, and its people. Caterpillar was one that caught my attention. In particular, I was attracted by the global nature of their business. I remember when their interviewer came on campus, and at the conclusion of our meeting, I asked him the question, "Is it really possible to experience the globe with a company like Caterpillar?" The interviewer responded, "Caterpillar is a company where, if you work hard and apply yourself, you can see the world and get paid to do it."

That was exactly what I did for 37 years. I started in Peoria, Illinois, and moved to San Francisco, California; Johannesburg, South Africa; Geneva, Switzerland; Raleigh, North Carolina; back to Peoria; to Singapore; and then, finally, back to Peoria again, until I retired in July 2016. In the span of close to four decades, I went from pricing individual piece parts to holding multiple positions in the Executive Office and becoming one of the CEO candidates of what, to me, will always be a great company. I loved my time at Caterpillar.

While I take great pride in what I achieved during my days at Caterpillar, it pales in comparison to the pride I take in my personal life. In 1981, I went in to get a new car loan, and I have now been married to the loan officer for more than 39 years. As I tell my wife, Ann, I traded in that car three years later, but I have been making payments ever since. However, the reality is that it is the best deal I ever cut. We went on to have three children, and we now have three in-laws and four grandsons. There is not a day that goes by that I do not reflect on the blessings of my family.

As I contemplated the possibilities of writing this book, I did question whether I had the credibility to share my views on how someone should live and lead. After much reflection, I decided it was worth sharing my views and experiences. The balance I had in my life enabled me to deal with the shock that comes from a projected life-ending diagnosis. Strong relationships have always played a key role in my personal and professional life, and they continue to do so today. Lastly, I have witnessed firsthand the results a dedicated and focused team can deliver, ranging from turning around challenged businesses to navigating through a global financial crisis to executing a large and complex ALS research initiative.

As you read the book, keep in mind you are reviewing the content through the lens of someone who went to one company, stayed for 37 years, worked in multiple divisions on four continents, and climbed the corporate ladder to the Executive Office of a Fortune 100 company. Someone who worked hard to find balance between his professional career and personal life. Someone who is dealing with a severe diagnosis and has found a way to remain positively engaged. Regardless of where you come from—a small town or another part of the world—or the challenges you face, you can apply these principles to live and lead effectively.

Balance

Perpetual devotion to what man calls his business is only to be sustained by perpetual neglect of many other things.

—Robert Louis Stevenson, Scottish writer

A well-designed flywheel needs to have the right mass located in the right place for it to turn at a high velocity. If, however, it goes out of balance, it wastes substantial energy on vibrations and the created forces can become destructive, thereby suboptimizing the flywheel's performance. This same principle applies to our personal lives. Pursuing a professional career at the expense of everything and everyone else can be a shallow victory.

When I took my first field assignment with Caterpillar, I felt I had a lot to prove because I had not come through the traditional career path in the field. I jumped into the job with both feet. I worked long hours and spent a lot of time on the road. Fortunately, I had a boss who cared not only about the business, but also about me. On one of his trips to my territory after he got an assessment of the work I was doing, he pulled me aside and shared his story.

Early in his career, he, too, was spending a lot of time on the road and working long hours. Once, he arrived home after a long trip, walked in on a heated discussion between his wife and daughter, and immediately injected himself into the conversation. Without getting all the details, he told his daughter how things needed to change. Out of frustration, his daughter responded, "Dad, sometimes it is just easier when you're not home." He was taken aback and advised me to not make the same mistake. Yes, getting ahead and making a difference in the job is important, but having a balance between work and home is equally so.

It was a lesson I never forgot, and throughout my career, it was the hardest part of the flywheel to maintain. While concurrent execution across the three principles of the flywheel is important, I start with balance for a reason. If you cannot lead yourself, are you prepared to lead others?

In our connected and nonstop world, perhaps the greatest challenge of leadership is finding a way to have it all—a great professional and personal life. According to the Bureau of Labor Statistics,[2] in 2019, the average American worked 44 hours per week, or 8.8 hours per day. However, in demanding industries like tech and finance, people clock over 60 hours a week as a rule and are available 24-7 by smartphone.[3] In 2020,[4] close to 50 percent of Americans considered themselves workaholics, 66 percent claimed they lacked work-life balance, and 77 percent experienced burnout at their current job. Given these statistics, it is clear that people have less downtime for themselves, spend less time with their families, and experience more stress and conflict, in general.

Some will contend this is the price of "success," but I do not buy it. Who do you want making critical decisions in your organization? Someone stressed about their health or relationships at home, or someone with good balance in their life? Trust me, balance is good for the individual, the business, and the shareholders.

Striking a balance among your chosen handful of critical priorities is likely the most important work you will ever do. You need a clear definition of winning or what *success* means to you. Working toward that will establish your purpose and help you align your actions. When you have clarity, you have less noise and stress to derail you. Of course, execution requires making choices and following them with ongoing discipline.

It is unrealistic to think you will find a perfect balance at all times, but knowing where you are relative to the balance you desire, is critical. To strike a balance, I suggest a three-pronged approach:

1. Make a plan. If you do not plan your personal life with the same rigor and discipline as your professional life, your personal life will suffer.
2. Efficiency will set you free. It is not about doing less work; it is about doing the work you do more efficiently.
3. Be a corporate athlete. To be ready for the competitive grind, you must be fit—physically, mentally, and emotionally.

Make a Plan

The first step is to step back and reflect. Most of us go with the flow, taking things as they come and waking up one day down the road wondering how we got to this place in life. We perform in a reactive mode, with no meticulous planning up front. It is amazing how much effort we put into our professional lives—strategy, vision/ mission, critical success factors, action items, values, and more. While we do a rather good job at all these, we forget the planning of "us." As outlined above, the harsh reality is, if you fail to plan your personal life with the same rigor and discipline as you do your professional life, your personal life will suffer.

Scott Peck,[5] author of the book *The Road Less Traveled*, says that by not planning, we tell ourselves that we are not important enough or do not love ourselves enough. If we love ourselves, we will take the time to plan our personal lives in exact detail.

You need to have a sense of direction regarding where you want to be in five or ten years. A key element of that plan is to articulate your personal vision, values, and practices.

Define Your Vision

Just as businesses have a defined vision supported by a strategy and actions, so must our personal lives. According to Stephen Covey,[6] author of *The 7 Habits of Highly Effective People*, defining a personal vision is the most important step you will take in your life.

Author Timothy Gallwey writes in *The Inner Game of Work*,[7] "If you have a clear vision of where you want to go, you are not as easily distracted by the many possibilities and agendas that otherwise divert you;" or, as my old boss, Bob Sulaski used to say, "Set a stake and run to it."

A clear vision inspires you to focus on what matters. It gives you a sense of direction, and all your decisions and actions begin to align with that. There is not a straight line from where you are to where you want to be, but with a sense of purpose and direction, every decision you make, whether at work or at home, should at least head you in the right direction.

This is the power of a personal vision. Do you have yours defined? If you do, that is great, and you are likely reaping the many benefits of that clarity. But if you do not, take the time to craft one now.

To begin, understand that your vision is unique to you. It is contingent upon your abilities, interests, values, aspirations, experiences, and defining elements of your current context. If you believe you have an average talent as a golfer, your vision probably should not be that of a golf professional, but do not be afraid to stretch yourself. The intent of putting a vision in place is to set a direction. It will help you navigate through noise or obstacles while maintaining clear focus on your goals.

Furthermore, your vision should encapsulate both work and personal goals. In other words, it must be synergistic in nature. In our connected and now-virtual world, it is almost impossible to draw a solid line between home and work. Before the advent of mobile devices, laptops, and the expectation of being "on" 24-7, one could disconnect when leaving the office, but this luxury has disappeared. Years ago, I used to do a lot of my reading on airplanes, but when laptops arrived, that time was partially taken up until the laptop battery died. Today, you can plug in your laptop and get nonstop access to Wi-Fi. Technology advancements continue to encroach upon your time and, unless managed, can become all-consuming. Getting ahead of this starts with a clear vision.

The process of envisioning is iterative. It requires repeated self-reflection. It may take a few rounds to write it, let alone perfect it. Begin by asking yourself the following questions:

"What kind of a life do I want to lead?"

"What is important to my family and me? And why?"

"What are my dreams?"

"What gives me joy?"

"What would I regret not doing?"

"At my retirement, what do I want people to say about me?"

"What do I want to be said in my eulogy or inscribed on my tombstone?"

On the tombstone, I would venture to guess it will not be, "I wish I had spent more time at the office," or "I wish I had worked harder for that promotion."

Jot down your answers to these questions. Let them be random and get you in the flow. Don't worry about the list getting too long. We are still in an ideation stage. Once you have exhausted your thoughts, review what you wrote and pick out consistent themes or patterns. What are the few words that stand out? Reflect on them and see if you identify with them or if they define who you want to be. Next, string them into a sentence or two (no more). Make them action-oriented, and you now have a draft of your vision.

Here are some examples[8] of vision statements to guide you:

> To be a teacher. And to be known for inspiring my students to be more than they thought they could be. (Oprah Winfrey)

> To have fun in [my] journey through life and learn from [my] mistakes. (Richard Branson)

> To positively impact the people and responsibilities experienced throughout life. (Mine)

Once they are written, mull over your statement. Look at it after a few days and see if it continues to resonate with you. Does it make sense and capture the essence of who you want to be? Does it excite you? Is it expressed in straightforward words? Tweak it if necessary.

The beauty of this exercise is that it articulates not only your life goals but also the challenges or trade-offs you may have to make to get there. If your vision is to rise to an executive level of your company, then that should give you an idea of how many miles you will have to walk and the kind of choices you will have to make along the way.

Here is an example: One of the high-potential leaders in my organization wanted to remain in North Carolina and not take opportunities that would require a physical move. He was aware that his decision would preclude him from several opportunities for growth and promotion, but clearly, those were not his goals in life. For him, the stability of his family and supporting his community were of utmost importance. Now, he was not the only one who chose something else over his career. I know of many who have turned down greater responsibility, gone part-time, or changed their career trajectories to follow their passions or to spend more time with their families and communities. I know of others who have chosen career over family. The key takeaway here is that there is no one right answer. Your vision will be unique to your circumstances and hence govern the choices and decisions you make.

Before you go on to execution, make it a shared vision. It is more powerful and doable if agreed upon and supported by the most important people in your life. Make sure your spouse, partner, children, and others are on board with your vision. Share with them what you want to achieve, why it is important to you, what is in it for them, and how they can support you through the process. They may also see gaps or possibilities that you may have missed. You will need support on your journey, and engaging your support system is essential in the process.

For dual-career couples, this is all the more critical. According to the Bureau of Labor Statistics,[9] more than 60% of married couples with children have dual careers. With or without children, the advantages of a dual-career house are significant, including greater financial stability and a chance for both partners to pursue career fulfillment. However, it is not without its challenges, and a key step in overcoming those challenges is to be in sync on the long-term plan.

Agree on the Values

After articulating your vision, define your personal/family values to achieve that vision. They are the *how*, or guiding principles, similar to the values attached to a corporate strategy.

Here are the Rapp family values:

- *Self-esteem.* We build self-esteem.
- *Honesty.* We always tell the truth.
- *Faith.* We are faithful to our God and family.
- *Competitive spirit.* We try hard and play fair.
- *Respect.* We respect one another and those in authority.
- *Responsibility.* We meet our commitments and fulfill our responsibilities.

Many of these were developed when our children were young. Self-esteem was critical in building their character. Honesty emphasized the importance of telling the truth. Faith was part of the introduction of belief to our children. Their competitive spirit was shaped by what we expected as they played sports. Respect was initially focused on their teachers (who deserved far more respect than they usually got). Responsibility was one we leveraged on teaching them to do their chores around the house.

I taught Sunday school with my wife, and we felt it was important to set the tone for the classroom. The first exercise was always to identify the "values" of the class. To get our pupils thinking, we would tell them they had just landed on the moon and had the freedom to define what values they wanted to live by at Sunday school. They would then start listing things important to them. This served as the framework to teach the class, and we would hold them accountable to those values.

Now it is your turn. Identify your guiding principles or values that will be the cornerstone of how you intend to execute your vision. Your values must be real and tied directly to your family's beliefs. Furthermore, they need to be in simple, easy-to-understand language. They cannot simply be bumper stickers or something that only has a social appeal. Bear in mind that clear vision and values stand the test of time. While your North Star (vision and values) should remain the same and only deviate in extreme circumstances, the action items to achieve them may change from time to time. While setting your vision and values is critical, this must be supported by actions or practices leading to change. The following are some practices that helped me on my journey.

Set Your Personal Calendar

To realize your vision, you must manage your calendar proactively. Like many, you may not have full latitude with your calendar. There are likely important meetings, your boss's priorities, or major events that you cannot avoid or change. But after planning the "must-dos" of work, turn to planning the "must-dos" of your personal life. Plan for the times when you can get the family together or take vacations. If you do not get ahead of your calendar, it will fill up, and then you will wonder why you are left with unused vacation days. If someone came into my office toward the end of the year and said, "I have been so busy I haven't had time to take any vacation," my response would not be, "You are such a hard worker," but rather, "You need to do a better job of planning your priorities and calendar."

Nothing happens without a solid plan, and managing your calendar is a huge part of that plan. Personally, I would plan my calendar a year in advance. Now, this is not to say changes did not occur, but for the most part, I maintained the discipline. I chose my priorities at home and work and ensured I fulfilled them both. As an example, I would calendar my family vacations early in the year. I always chose weeks of major holidays (Easter, Memorial Day, Fourth of July, etc.), where I could take four days off and get a complete week, which also often corresponded to when the children were off from school.

This is not just about vacations. Map everything that is important to you: exercise, children's activities, or special days, such as birthdays, anniversaries, prom nights, or something else that deserves your presence and time. You may not always be there, but if you fail to plan ahead, you will surely miss them all. Do not believe your children or spouse when they say it does not matter if you miss an event—they all matter. If you cannot be there, make sure they know you are thinking about them.

Dinner With the Family

President Ronald Reagan was a great champion of the power of family dinners. In his farewell address to the nation, he declared, "All great change in America begins at the dinner table. So tomorrow night in the kitchen, I hope the talking begins." If the President of the United States believed in and made time for a nightly family dinner, you can too.

While living in Geneva, I often had teleconferences with the States that would run well into the evenings. If a call was scheduled to be over at 7:00 p.m. and was dragging on, I would simply say, "I have a dinner obligation outside the office. Is there anything else you need from me?" Now, most of the time, the obligation was dinner at home. Why would I not show the same respect for my family as I would to a dealer, supplier, or customer? Ann had a very straightforward approach. She would say, "I can only hold the kids off for dinner until 7:00 p.m. If you need more time at the office, I completely understand. Go in at 4:00 a.m.!"

Eating dinner together is not for the sake of it; there is a lot more to this ritual. In one study, Marla Eisenberg and her team[10] from University of Minnesota studied the link between frequency of family meals and substance use, academic performance, self-esteem, depressive symptoms, suicidal ideation, and suicide attempts in a sample of about five thousand adolescents. The findings revealed family mealtime to be a potential protective factor in the lives of adolescents for nearly all these variables. Also, the frequency of family meals was inversely associated with tobacco, alcohol, and marijuana use, low grade point average, depressive symptoms, and suicide. Clearly, there are numerous benefits of eating meals together. Not only do you nurture well-behaved children, but this also permeates into your leadership and work efficiencies. Think about it: if you have stability and peace at home, you will perform better at work.

To keep the communication channel open within the family during dinnertime, we used highs and lows, the best and worst things that happened today. If you ask your children, "What did you do today?" they will likely say, "Nothing." If you ask them, "How was school?" they will say, "Fine." However, if you ask what was the best and worst thing that happened to them today, it opens up the discussion. Yes, sometimes this was painful for us. Our most difficult move was from Geneva to Raleigh, and for six months our two daughters' low was, "We live in North Carolina." Yes, it was hard to hear, but at least we knew where things stood and that we needed to do everything we could to make it a successful transition for them.

One of the practices we utilized to strike a balance between home and work was to have work colleagues to the house for dinner. If a customer or Caterpillar colleague was traveling in on business and a dinner was involved, I would often suggest they come home and have dinner with us. I would warn them in advance that it would include our children. A side benefit of this practice was that our children learned to engage with older adults at a very young age, and it also built closer relationships with those who came into our home.

There are other concepts to make your family dinners more engaging. Follow the 10:50:1 rule put forward by Bruce Feiler in his book *The Secrets of Happy Families*:[11]

- *Ten minutes of quality talk.* Researchers found that ten minutes is about the amount of quality talk time an average meal yields. That is not much, but a little regularly each day adds up over time.
- *Let your child speak 50% of the time.* Adults usually talk for two-thirds of that ten-minute conversation time. While there are benefits for children in overhearing adult conversations, you also want to hear what they have to say. Encourage them to speak up. It is a great training ground for them to practice speaking and holding a conversation.
- *One new word every meal.* Studies indicate that children who have regular family mealtimes have larger vocabularies than those who do not. But holding regular family dinners does not magically teach new words; you have to be intentional. At dinner every day, the author Bruce Feiler taught his children one new word by playing different games. For example, he would throw out a word like *fruit* and then have everyone come up with as many related words as possible. You can get as creative as you want.

A final suggestion: Keep mobile devices, including Mom's and Dad's, away from the dinner table and understand that a family dinner does not involve TV trays with the TV on. Put a basket or a charging station on the counter near the dining table. Make it a habit to put your phone, as well as those of your children, in the basket before you sit down for dinner. Yes, initially it will be difficult, but soon it will become a habit.

The above are just some ideas to jump-start your dinner routine. You can decide how you want to engage everyone during mealtimes and beyond. The real benefit is the opportunity for the family to slow down, get together face-to-face, share, strengthen values, garner support, and build strong bonds.

Hobbies and Fun Activities

Balance is not just about work and home; it is also about your personal time—to have fun, unwind, and recoup your energies. However, in the wake of technology and smart gadgets, we have forgotten how to spend time with ourselves. In fact, phones have replaced hobbies and other activities that were known to be stress busters or offered a space to recover and restore. These diversions not only facilitate individual well-being but also nurture relationships, clarity of thought, and optimal performance.

According to a 2015 study[12] conducted by scholars Zawadzki, Smyth, and Costigan from the University of California and The Pennsylvania State University, participants who engaged in leisure activities were found to be happier, less bored, and less stressed. They had lower heart rates. They also demonstrated increased productivity and job performance as the activities boosted creativity and gave the brain a much-needed break to recharge. Similarly, Sarah Pressman and colleagues[13] found that engaging in hobbies and/or sports, socializing, or spending time in nature resulted in less fatigue as well as lower blood pressure, cortisol, waist circumference, and body mass index, and perceptions of better physical function. Clearly, downtime is a key part of your balance and eventual success.

Cultivate hobbies if you have none. They serve as a cathartic outlet to your daylong work. Better still, involve your family in those. While I have always enjoyed golf, I gave it up for ten years. When I was working in Geneva and traveling a lot, the last thing I wanted to do when I came home for the weekend was to spend Saturdays on the golf course. So I gave up the game, and while my golf game went downhill, my downhill skiing greatly improved. Almost every Saturday during the winter months, we headed to the mountains to ski. There is nothing comparable to sitting on a chairlift with your family in the midst of the beauty of the mountains. Yes, we brought up our children around the world and away from immediate family, but times like those in the mountains made us a very close "family of five."

Remember Your Significant Other

Every relationship needs time and nurturance. Marriage is no different. It is so easy for us to get caught up in day-to-day work and chores that marriage can quickly take a back seat. When relationships suffer, work life, or, rather, life, suffers! A seventy-year-old study led by George Vaillant[14] at Harvard University found that at age 50, healthy aging is better predicted by a good marriage than by low cholesterol levels. Those in less-conflicted marriages lived longer and healthier lives than unmarried individuals, according to a study by psychologists Roger Kaplan and Richard Kronick[15] at the University of California in Los Angeles and San Diego, respectively.

Spending time together can take the shape of simply talking about each other's day, listening, offering support, or being empathic. Going out for special dates, dinner, or events is equally worthwhile. You may be thinking these are good ideas, but where is the time? This is where the crux of managing work and home pivots.

I was deliberate in carving out my time with my wife, Ann. I knew it was important because she went to great lengths to take care of everything around the house so I could dedicate time to the children when I was home. When in Geneva, Ann and I would catch an early bus downtown on Saturday mornings. We would go to our favorite coffee shop for coffee and croissants. It gave us time to get caught up and for Ann to download on all that had gone on during the week. Then we would walk Old Town, strolling through the shops, and finish at the farmer's market. We would buy cheese, fresh bread, fruit, and vegetables and then head home for a long, casual lunch with our family. It was really a great way to spend time as a couple.

To plan your time together, decide how many times a month you want "together time" or a date night. Put it on your calendar so you remain committed to it. Another way to do this is to leverage weekend mornings, when your children are sleeping in late. Get up early, go out for a stroll, coffee, or something else nice. By the time you come back, the children may just be waking up. If you prefer not to go out, stay at home and enjoy quiet moments. If it is the evenings you find most appealing, arrange for a babysitter or ask a friend to watch the children.

While going out on date nights is certainly one way to spend time together, doing household chores is another option. Sociologist Daphne Stevens[16] from Utah State University found that the more men are involved in household chores, the better women rate their marriages. Whether it is doing dishes, folding laundry, or cooking, seek those opportunities to form a deeper connection with your spouse or partner.

Strong relationships are the foundation of a strong family unit. No amount of family vision is going to help if the foundation is weak and shaky. Creating meaningful experiences, showing genuine interest, and prioritizing each other are all simple, daily actions that you can take right now to find that balance in your busy life. In the words of Theodore Hesburgh, "The most important thing a father can do for his children is to love their mother, and vice versa."

In summary, a key component of finding balance in your life starts with "making a plan." It is an explicit way of defining who you want to be and putting the values and actions in place to give yourself a fighting chance. In the absence of a plan, you run the risk of reflecting back on your life and wondering how it turned out the way it did. Avoid this regret by making a plan now.

Efficiency Will Set You Free

The second area of focus relative to balance is driving efficiencies in your life. My perspective on eliminating waste from my life was influenced by the lean principles taught as part of the Caterpillar Production System (CPS). Every manufacturing process has waste. And so do our personal lives.

In this section, I talk about applying those very principles to building efficiencies at work and at home. How do we eliminate the waste that exists in our lives? My premise is that a balanced life does not come from doing less work but from doing the work you do more efficiently. In many cases, we have the time; we just fail to use it efficiently.

Review the areas highlighted below to take a "mental waste walk-through" of your own practices and habits. Hopefully, they will trigger thoughts on opportunities to build efficiencies in your life.

Meetings

When working in Geneva, I had the good fortune to work with a great administrative assistant, Monique Colloca. My schedule was a challenge. I traveled extensively, and when I was in the office, I was in back-to-back meetings, leaving little time to think or work on important things. Monique decided there had to be a better way. She started with the premise that, with the exception of staff or strategy meetings, all others would be 30 minutes long. When someone called for time on my calendar, the discussion with Monique was along the lines of, "I need an hour with Ed." Monique would respond, "He only has 30 minutes." If they said they needed more time, Monique would say, "Please send your topic and recommendations in advance, and Ed will review them prior to the meeting." If they responded that they did not have a summary or recommendation, Monique would reply, "Are you sure you are ready for a meeting with Ed?"

As leaders, we can all do a better job of setting an expectation of completed staff work. To free up your time, avoid becoming forgiving in this expectation. Expect an agenda up front, material shared prior, a clear recommendation; conclude with a "who's going to do what and by when" discussion. Too often, the only summary is to agree to another meeting—not a good use of time.

Beware of unplanned, impromptu meetings. Do you have colleagues who only stop by to visit? Does that seem to happen when you have the most to do? One can be as social as anyone else when it comes to building relationships with colleagues, but when they merely want to pass time, listen for a bit, and then simply stand up. Nine times out of ten, they will get the cue and also get up and prepare to leave. It is not that we want to be rude. Remember, we are trying to find time to better manage our lives.

Email

When email first became part of our personal and professional lives, we loved the sound and sight of emails dropping in our inbox. Do you recall those days?

Today, email has gone to another extreme. There are too many emails. A Harvard study[17] found that an executive receives an average of 200 emails a day. An average employee checks emails 74 times a day and spends 13 hours, or 28% of the workweek, on emails. Clearly, it takes away a big chunk of productive time from our lives.

To manage the avalanche of pouring emails, I always tried to follow a four-step process—File, Forward, Action, or Delete. Yes, after going through this filter, there are a few that will remain in your inbox but not nearly as many. On File, set up a simple email filing structure. A measure of success is how long it takes you to find a document. The more structured your approach, the easier it will be. On "Forward," make sure you explicitly state what you want done with the email. Are you forwarding on an FYI basis, or does it require action? Put it in the subject line and be clear. On "Action," make the decision on what you want to do. Yes, some will require more time and thought, but email should be used for brief topics, not heavy-duty proposals. Lastly, on "Delete," I would hate to think about how many emails get stored instead of deleted. If they require no action or future reference, just hit the Delete button. Avoid hoarding them for a rainy day.

Keep your email responses short and to the point—brevity is king. If you get an email with a request or recommendation, a "Forge ahead" or "Works for me" response is fine. Find a routine that works for you to keep your emails clean. Like texts, you can clean them first thing in the morning, around noon, and then in the evening. This was something I struggled to do, but writing this book brought it back to the forefront. If I put my telephone away, I focused and made progress. If it was close at hand, I was constantly interrupted by email notifications or text messages.

Bottom line: Taking control of your time starts by being in control of your email. If you do not put some structure around your email habits, you will spend all your time watching your inbox, with no time left for strategic issues.

Travel Time

When on the road, be on the job as any work completed on the road frees up time for the family when you get back home. Whether it is in airports, airplanes, or hotels, make the most of the time. It is amazing how people can complain about not having any free time, and then they watch two movies on an international flight instead of getting their work done. Load reading material onto your iPad; surf your calendar in advance to prepare for upcoming meetings and presentations.

When I announced my retirement, a dear friend and colleague, Stu Levenick, who had previously retired, reached out and said, "You are never going to know the treadmill you are on until you get off." Several months into retirement, I knew exactly what he meant. For 25 years, I had traveled hard, being away for at least part of nearly every week. I remain a big believer in "showing up," but there is no doubt the pandemic has shown us we can augment face-to-face contact with Zoom, Teams, and other tools. When on the road, make the most of your time. While I loved what I did for work, my favorite part of every trip was coming home, and the more efficient I was on the road, the more I could be present when I returned.

Outsourcing

I remember teaching a work-life balance class at a Harvard executive management program with a renowned author, Richard Leider. He taught the theory, and I taught the practical applications in daily life. As we went into a joint Q&A at the end of the presentation, a young woman said, "This all sounds good, but my husband and I both have busy careers. How are we supposed to make it work?"

I reminded her of one of my opening comments—your only defense is a good offense—and at a minimum, I suggested making two practices a priority. First, have dinner as a family whenever possible, and secondly, outsource everything that you do not love to do around the house. Having two daughters of my own, I am sensitive to the heavy burden carried by female leaders. On the one hand, they are expected to compete and lead in their professional lives, but on the other, they also carry the majority of the load in their personal lives.

Anything you do not love to do or that does not add value should be a candidate for outsourcing. Not only does this option take pressure off you, but it also gives you quality time to spend on things that do matter to you. For myself, I chose not to mow our lawn. For years I paid a landscaper to take care of our yard. It was not that I did not enjoy yard work, but with a heavy travel schedule, I did not want my weekends interrupted for yard work over family time.

I do acknowledge outsourcing comes with a price. So be prudent in starting small and seeing how it frees up your time. It may prove to be worth the investment in your family and career.

Technology Management

To free up time, you can eliminate waste or increase productivity. Often, we turn to technology to enhance productivity in the hope of a better balanced life. However, many times, and despite all the possibilities that come with technology, we have not seen it translate into higher levels of productivity. It has only increased by 1 to 2% per year, according to the U.S. Bureau of Labor Statistics.[18] Now, this is not a surprise to many experts. Constant interruptions or switching from one task to another block performance and productivity.

A study led by Gloria Mark[19] from the University of California-Irvine shows that it can take us about 23 minutes to get back to a task after an interruption. When you consider the average executive receives 46 smartphone notifications a day, as per a study by research firm Dscout,[20] that suggests that most executives never spend any time in flow mode at all. Instead of remaining focused on key issues, they are constantly interrupted. Recent estimates find that while each task switch might waste only a minuscule of a second, it can add up to a 40% productivity loss.

Technology usage left unchecked can have a devastating effect on our well-being. According to an *Irish Times* article,[21] 57% of families say technology has ruined their family dinnertime. By design, technology is developed to catch your attention and increase your screen time. The dings and banners, the light coming on with a message, and the vibrations are all meant to do just that. Experts developing the applications are constantly innovating in more and more ways to engage you and your children.

If you have not watched the Netflix documentary *The Social Dilemma*, take the time to do so. Staying connected with your family is getting more difficult as apps are focused on capturing attention. Edward Tufte, a Yale professor said, "There are only two industries that call their customers 'users'—drugs and technology."

To better manage technology, turn off your notifications. Turn off the beep or vibrate setup on your phones when an email or text comes in—we are not trained monkeys. Be on the high ground to decide when you want to interact with this tool. Allocate specific time windows when you will look at your telephone, laptop, or iPad. At other times, keep them away and out of sight, because the mere sight of the phone, even when turned off or in your pocket, is distracting. In a study at the University of Texas-Austin, Adrian Ward and colleagues[22] found that participants who had their telephones in a different room significantly outperformed those with phones on their desks, and slightly outperformed those who had kept them in a pocket or handbag.

Consider it a test to see if you can control your life instead of having technology control you. On the positive front, leverage apps that improve productivity. A couple of them are Priorities (where I log all to-dos and track follow-ups) and Occasions (where I log all special occasions).

In closing on "efficiency," do a "waste walk" through the last month and evaluate your calendar, use of technology, and opportunities to outsource. If you look closely, I am convinced you will find multiple opportunities to free up time to improve balance and productivity in your life. Remember, good balance is not about doing less work but about doing the work you do more effectively and efficiently.

Be a Corporate Athlete

Planning your personal life with the same rigor and discipline as your professional life and driving efficiencies in the way you live and lead will take you toward finding balance in your life. However, I would offer that a third step is required—you need to be a corporate athlete to secure the full benefits.

There is nothing outlined in the discussion below that will come as a surprise to you. If we eat well, exercise, get our required sleep, and stay mentally sharp, we will feel and perform better. As Wayne Fields said in his nursery rhyme,

> The best six doctors anywhere,
> And no one can deny it,
> Are sunshine, water, rest and air,
> Exercise, and diet.
> These six will gladly you attend
> If only you are willing.
> Your mind they'll ease;
> Your will they'll mind
> And charge you not a shilling.

While this is obvious, as a society we are failing to integrate many of these practices into our daily routine. We have succumbed to fast-paced lives and complain about working ourselves "to death" in an attempt to "have it all."

Scholars Leslie Perlow and Jessica Porter[23] from Harvard Business School found that 94% of working professionals work more than 50 hours per week, and almost half say they put in 65 or more hours per week. That does not include the 20–25 hours a week most of them spend monitoring their phones while outside the office. They also always respond within an hour of receiving a message from a colleague or a client. With this as a routine, where is the time for rest, exercise and the family?

A study conducted by Indiana University's Kelley School of Business found that workers in "high-demand" jobs are 15.4% more likely to die before those with low job demands. According to the lead researcher, Erik Gonzalez-Mulé,[24] when you lack the necessary resources—physical, mental, or emotional—to deal with a demanding job, you cultivate other habits. You begin to ignore yourself. You eat more, smoke, or indulge in other vices to combat stress. The message here is that in order to give your best performance, you need to be physically and mentally fit.

In 2001, Dr. Jim Loher, co-founder of Johnson & Johnson Human Performance Institute, and Tony Schwartz, CEO and founder of the Energy Project, a consulting firm, transferred the fundamentals of professional athlete performances to the business world. They found that athletes invest a significant amount of time in training and resting for optimal performance. The reverse, however, is true for the rest of us—nonstop work, no downtime, and high expectations. In fact, the demands we face in our average day are far more challenging than those any professional athletes have to face in their careers.

Professional Athletes	Corporate Professionals
Generally, spend 90% of their time training in order to perform 10% of the time.	Spend at least 90% of their time performing and, if lucky, 10% training.
Have Olympic-quality nutrition, sleep, exercise, psychological support, and rest.	Work long hours in stressful circumstances, often with poor nutrition and sleep.
Typically enjoy an "off-season" of 4–5 months a year (depending on the sport).	Have an "off-season" of a few weeks' vacation that includes checking emails and calling in for meetings.
An average career span of 5–10 years and enough savings for a lifetime.	A career span of 40–50 years.

Are you one of the statistics outlined above? Take a moment to do a self-assessment.

- Are you at your target weight?
- Does your daily routine include a balanced diet and exercise?
- Do you have great energy to engage with the family after work?
- Do you get enough sleep?
- Do you practice methods to stay mentally fit?

If the answers to these questions are a resounding "yes," then you are in good shape. But if not, let us focus on some basic steps to get you moving in the right direction. The following sections highlight elements of a basic training platform: diet, exercise, sleep, and mental relaxation.

Diet

After my ALS diagnosis, I decided to become even more disciplined regarding my diet, and I have followed the Wahls Protocol for the past six years. In an early discussion with Dr. Wahls, I told her that following her protocol was going to be difficult. Her response was, "What kind of car do you drive?" At that time, I was driving an Audi A7, and she asked, "Do you ever put anything other than premium fuel in it?" Of course, my answer was no. Her response: "Why do you treat your car better than yourself?"

Unfortunately, as a society, we are not using premium fuel. Obesity is becoming a major health risk and is trending in the wrong direction. The average American has put on at least fifteen pounds over the last 20 years according to a report by the US Centers for Disease Control (CDC) and Prevention's National Center for Health Statistics.[25] This is not only happening to adults but to children as well. Eleven-year-old girls gained an average of seven pounds during the period researchers analyzed, while boys gained more than thirteen pounds.

My intent is not to preach but to simply have you assess where you stand versus these statistics. If you need to improve the quality of fuel you are using, deploy some of these recommended steps:

- Eat breakfast. According to an old saying, "Have breakfast like a king, lunch like a prince, dinner like a pauper." If you are like most, you actually do it in the opposite order. Get your day off to a good start with a good breakfast.
- Eat between meals. Consume a healthful snack of fruits, vegetables, or nuts before and after lunch for a steady flow of glucose and energy levels. When the time comes for your regimented meals, you are not famished or so out of control that you eat anything and everything put in front of you. Eating right is about making healthful eating the easiest possible option. To ensure you do this, stock your home and office with the "right" food choices.
- Eat lunch with your colleagues/friends, away from your desk. According to Jennifer Newman, a workplace psychologist, eating together builds relationships that nurture support systems. Workplace satisfaction is much higher if you eat with colleagues, suggests a study conducted by Brian Wansink,[26] the director of Cornell University's Food and Brand Lab, and his team. They found significant positive correlations between work performance and eating together.
- Whenever possible, have dinner with your family. As discussed earlier, it is good not only for you but for your family as well. Dinners offer an opportunity for the family to come together, share their highs and lows, strengthen ties, and build better relationships. Correlational data shows that families that eat together have stronger marital bonds and better-adjusted children. In a sample of about 1,300 youths, Jayne Fulkerson[27] from the school of nursing at the University of Minnesota, and colleagues, found that family connectedness, prioritization of family meals, and positive

mealtime environments were significantly associated with a better psychological well-being of the family.

- Drink in moderation. While I enjoyed a glass of wine as much as anyone else, I was very disciplined, especially in the work environment. Never in my career did I have too much to drink in a work setting. My approach was simple: At a cocktail party, it was always club soda with a twist of lime, as I simply wanted to avoid a discussion of "Don't you drink?" Then at dinner, it was one glass of wine.

In short, make your meals a priority and be disciplined about eating right and watching what you drink. As you sit down for a meal, just ask yourself, "Am I taking in premium fuel?"

As for any athlete in training, the right diet has to be supported by a good exercise routine. Sustained high performance in the face of ever-increasing pressure and rapid change requires a fit and agile body. Like professional athletes, corporate athletes need regular exercise to sharpen their physical and mental faculties.

Exercise

Today, more than ever, exercise is a necessary requirement for efficient functioning. Our bodies were created to be on the move always, hunting and gathering. Those days have been replaced by sedentary lives, where we sit at our desks, commute in cars, sit on airplanes, take elevators to go up and down, sit in front of televisions, and do everything to minimize effort in the name of convenience and comfort. The result, if not addressed, will make us more fatigued and increase our health risks.

Exercise is a must to feel good and be efficient in what you do. A study by Frank Penedo and Jason Dahn[28] from University of Miami, Florida, shows a positive link between physical activity and better quality of life and health outcomes. The more you work out, the better you feel. Exercise increases the production of neurotransmitters, muscles, strength, and more that are beneficial for your overall functioning. Additionally, a Mayo Clinic report shows that exercise prevents weight gain, buffers you from illness, raises immunity, improves mood, boosts energy, lowers stress, improves sex drive, promotes better sleep, facilitates social connections, and is simply fun to engage in. In the words of Chris Crowley and Henry Lodge, authors of *Younger Next Year* (one of my favorite books),[29] "Exercise keeps the body in a growth mode and in its absence, puts you in a 'decay' mode."

There are many emotional and cognitive benefits as well. A Stanford University study by Candice Hogan, Jutta Mata, and Laura Carstensen[30] showed how physical activity is associated with improved affective experience and enhanced cognitive processing. Moderate exercise in their sample was linked with increased levels of positive affect, such as feeling alert and active. There was improved concentration, sharper memory, faster learning, mental stamina, enhanced creativity, and lower stress among those who exercised. Similarly, a study by Lindsay Hoyt[31] of the University of California-Berkeley showed that high positive arousal or excitement because of exercise is linked to a steeper decline in cortisol levels throughout the day.

As a leader, I always felt being a corporate athlete was required to do my job. I ran global organizations that spanned multiple time zones for the last fifteen years of my career. I was always sensitive to the fact that when I engaged with employees, dealers, suppliers, or customers around the world, they couldn't care less about my jet lag or work schedule or other priorities I was juggling. They rightfully expected me to be engaged, interested in their issues, and at the top of my game. I believed that, for me to do this, I had to be a corporate athlete. Exercise, as a key part of that, allowed me to be energized, driven, emotionally stable, and mentally alert to deal with daily situations.

When it comes to the time to build your exercise routine, I believe morning is the best time. There are too many excuses in the evening: "I'm tired," "I want to be with the family," "I have errands to run," "I have dinner with a client," etc. The only excuse in the morning is, "I was too lazy to get up." All through the years that I exercised in the morning, there was never a time that I got up early to exercise when later I wished I had stayed in bed.

Expectedly, there can be barriers to a consistent exercise routine. Top on the list are competing demands on our time. There are always commitments that tend to take precedence. We delegate exercise to a secondary position: We will exercise when we have the time or after we finish work. Outcome: We never have the time. For some people, consistent exercise follows a health scare when it becomes doctor's orders. I would suggest you get ahead of this in an effort to avoid poor health in the first place. For me, the goal was to live to be one hundred and spoil my grandchildren. I did not want to go through my career and use up my physical and mental energy and then be a tired and worn-out retiree. I wanted to come out in good shape. For this very reason, I tried to exercise a minimum of five days a week.

My exercise routine was built around three principles:

1. I converted an area in the house into an exercise space. I would hate to guess what percent of gym memberships go unused in this country. I wanted to remove the multiple excuses of "It takes too much time," "The gym is not on my way to work," or "I don't want to have to shower and take a change of clothes." My home workout space was a two-minute walk from my bedroom. While some cringe at the cost of exercise equipment, I believe it is cheaper than an unused gym membership.

2. A morning routine: Exercise in the morning, for there are too many excuses in the evening. I set a 5:00 a.m. alarm for the vast majority of my professional career. As I said before, there was never a day I got up and exercised when later I wished I had stayed in bed.

3. Muscle confusion: In the early days, I was a runner. But I soon realized the power of muscle confusion. I rotated cardio, weights, and yoga to get a comprehensive workout. The book *Younger Next Year* does a great job of laying out why you need muscle confusion.

Here are a few additional points to consider as you develop your own exercise plan: First of all, if it involves something you love to do, then all the better. For me, that was downhill skiing, walking while playing golf, and full-court basketball with my son and friends. When you can match the benefits of exercise with the joy of something you like to do, it is a good match. Secondly, this is one place where peer pressure can help. Having a friend, spouse, colleague, or technology hold you accountable is good. When we lived in California, two other men in the neighborhood and I would meet at a designated stoplight at 5:30 every morning for a run. We all agreed that if any one of us was in town and failed to show up, the other two had the right to go knock on his door. Needless to say, waking up the wife and kids was not a good option. This type of peer pressure holds you accountable and keeps you moving forward. Today, through technology like the Apple Watch or Fitbit, you can be held virtually accountable.

At the end of the day, it is simple math. While there are numerous diet plans and apps, I firmly believe it is a combination of diet, exercise, and tracking (holding yourself accountable). You execute a plan, and the outcomes are in front of you. If you do not, the consequences are still in front of you. You decide which result appeals to you more.

Sleep

For most of us, sleep is the first thing to suffer when we have a lot on our plate. I was guilty of this for years, until I was instructed by my neurologist that I had to get more sleep. It did not affect my ability to function, but my doctor convinced me it could affect my health in the long run.

We can blame it on external factors, but we are sleeping less and less. In fact, according to a National Sleep Foundation research,[32] 29% of people claim to feel sleepy at work, and 30% have admitted falling asleep behind the wheel. When we are sleep-deprived, there are significant consequences. We are tired, unfocused, unproductive; we make mistakes and deliver inferior work.

To avoid these pitfalls, experts recommend seven to nine hours of quality sleep. Admittedly, this range can vary for each of us, but the common message is that you need to feel rested and fresh every day. It is during sleep that the body cleanses, consolidates, strengthens, and stabilizes neural memory and feeds creative thinking and performance. Some science-backed suggestions include the following:

- Sleeping and awakening at the same time every day
- Exercising
- Consuming more bright daylight during the day
- Not eating or drinking within three hours of bedtime
- Turning off technology at least 30 minutes before going to bed
- Documenting gratitude
- Practicing mindfulness

Once I understood the importance of sleep, I changed my habits to get eight hours of sleep a night. The change came about like all other changes—it was simply a matter of forming a new habit that allowed for the extra sleep, and I flexed on both ends, going to bed a bit earlier and getting up a bit later. If you want a more detailed explanation of the benefits of sleeping, read *Why We Sleep* by Matthew Walker.

In wrapping up the discussion on physical fitness, whether it concerns eating right, exercising, or getting enough sleep, pick an app like MyFitnessPal. In phase 1, get into the habit (more on habits later) of loading the data, as it all starts with awareness. Then, set your target weight and by when you want to achieve it (do not get too aggressive), and it will solve for the combination of calories and/or exercise (remember, this is just math). Finally, do not forget to track your performance and how you are inching toward your target.

While the above plan is designed to get you physically fit, a corporate athlete also must focus on building a strong mind.

Mental Fitness

The last element of the training platform is mental fitness. The mind is the motherboard for what we do—how, when, and why. For best-in-class functioning, it has to be in the prime of health. Given the constant stimuli and information with which we are bombarded, it is not always easy to keep calm and focused. Our mind flutters from one thing to another, trying to make sense of the myriad of stimuli in front of us. Perhaps this is one aspect of health that has been most affected by the pandemic, as we have lost control over our own mental fitness. Working from home, staring at the screen, avoiding social interactions, and adapting to the new normal have taken a toll on our well-being.

To be in control of your mind and proficient at what you do, scientists reinforce several tactics.

Filter Information

Data[33] show that in 2009, an average American consumed 34 gigabytes of content and 100,000 words of information every day. Most consumed 11.8 hours of information a day—watching television and computer screens, interacting with the phone, radio, and print. With the advent of social media, the Global Index says we are spending, on an average, more than two hours on social networks alone. This information overload, which typically is irrelevant, not only takes time away from important tasks but also induces cognitive fatigue, whereby one is tired with the load of processing and assimilating such an avalanche of information.

To avoid this fatigue, consume information smartly. A *USA Today* study[34] measured the amount of time between the snap of the ball and blowing of the whistle in an NFL football game. While it takes three hours to watch, the actual playing time is eleven minutes and 42 seconds. Though it is a personal choice, DVR and YouTube summaries are all efficient ways to consume such events. Filtering out certain portals or removing apps is another way to avoid temptation. In fact, you can set up downtime on your devices, during which you will receive no updates or information to disturb you.

To save time, develop and apply a filter on what you consume and how. Be intentional and mindful of what you watch, listen to, or read.

Be Grateful

Perhaps the best few days I spent in my career were with Ed Foreman, who taught the "Successful Life Course." Many of the concepts in this book were born out of my time with Ed. He laid out a protocol that led to habits, and one of them concerned my outlook on each and every day. When you see people, often their first question is, "How are you doing?" The traditional, automatic response is, "Fine. How are you?" Ed taught me to change my response to, "Every day is a terrific day." Yes, some are more terrific than others, but I keep life in perspective. This is not about fooling yourself into believing life is good. I have traveled into the bowels of Africa, India, Russia, and other parts of the world, and trust me, for many of us, life indeed is terrific.

"Grateful" is on my calendar every day at 5:00 p.m. It is a constant reminder for me to reflect on all the things I have to be grateful for. I developed this habit after taking the Yale University online course called the Science of Well-Being, taught by Professor Laurie Santos. She emphasizes that one of our challenges is that our minds' strongest intuitions are often wrong. The mind always wants to compare to others, and social media is making this a constant reminder, but it is not based on reality and only shows the good side—people rarely chat or post about the bad things in their lives. A big portion of the class is focused on being more mindful or aware of your positive surroundings, the things to be grateful for.

The act of appreciation, or being thankful, stimulates two important regions in our brain, one of which regulates stress, and the other activates the brain's reward system. These evoke feelings of pleasure. According to psychologists Dr.

Robert Emmons, of the University of California-Davis, and Dr. Michael McCullough, of University of Miami,[35] there is a strong relationship between gratitude and well-being. In their study, they asked the participants to write a few sentences each week focusing on particular topics. One group wrote about things they were grateful for that had occurred during the week. A second group wrote about daily irritations or things that had bothered them, and the third wrote about events that had affected them. What they found was that after ten weeks, those who wrote about gratitude were not only more optimistic and felt better about their lives but also felt healthier than those who focused on sources of irritation.

To develop a habit of appreciating life, make reflecting on what you are grateful for a daily habit—put it on your calendar.

Practice MCR (Mind-Controlled Relaxation)

According to Ed Foreman, author of *The Power of Living by Design* and other books,[36] a few minutes of an intentional MCR can recapture your energy, vitality, and vibrancy. The idea behind this or any other mindfulness practice is to focus on the "now" and the "present" and avoid ruminating over the past or worrying about the future. As we do that, we are not physiologically stressed or anxious and hence not releasing cortisol, the stress hormone. Now, what does this relaxation practice look like? Here's an illustration based on Ed's teachings:

Close your eyes and visualize a place you think would relax you—being enveloped by the soft and warm sand of the beach, a cozy cottage in the mountains while enjoying the warmth of crackling fire, or somewhere else. As you mentally find yourself in that place, let go of all stress, drift along, and enjoy peace.

Inhale a deep breath of air. Let your lungs expand. Hold and slowly let it out. Enjoy peace and rest. As you feel calm, bring your thoughts to your toes, working upward to the top of your head. You begin to concentrate your focus on toes—relax them. Then move up to your feet, heels, ankles, calves, knees, thighs, hips, lower back, middle back, and upper back. Concentrate thoughts on your stomach—internally and externally. Chest is relaxed. There is a warm, tingling sensation in your hands, wrist, forearms, shoulders, neck, chin, lips, tongue, eyelids, forehead, cheeks—all are relaxed. Let go of anxiety and frustration. As you slowly visualize relaxing every part of your body, you will fall into a state of slumber. This is totally your time. Other things can wait. You are at peace and in tranquility.

Hold a vivid image of the healthy, happy, improved self you are becoming. Feeling confident, in charge, in control, getting healthier, happier, stronger.

I started doing this after attending Ed's program more than 20 years ago. Whether it was on the airplane or in the hotel, between meetings and dinner, I would close my eyes and practice it. Today, I do it at home, sitting in my office chair. Fifteen minutes of it revitalizes me for the balance of the day. By mentally slowing down, directing relaxation to your muscles and organs, and slowing down your heart rate, you can become adept at programming your body to the equivalent rejuvenation of a two-hour nap in approximately 15 minutes.

Being a corporate athlete requires integration of the basic elements of a training platform—diet, exercise, sleep, mental fitness. All I am trying to do is to raise awareness of where you stand in an effort to prompt action leading to your own training program.

Tying It All Together

In closing, perhaps one of the gifts of the pandemic is the realization that business leaders don't need to travel nonstop to do the job. Yes, showing up will still matter, but intuition tells me we will gravitate to a post-pandemic hybrid model, increasing the opportunities to find better balance. However, it will still be hard work, and it all starts with a plan.

On the importance of balance, I thought it best to have the message reinforced by someone who touches our daily lives, be it through our Mac, iPad, iPhone, Apple Watch, Apple TV, or the countless apps on our phone or watch. Steve Jobs had an incredible vision and reshaped the technology landscape. However, one of his last written documents was not about the job, technology, money, or success but about life:

> I reached the pinnacle of success in the business world. In some others' eyes, my life is the epitome of success. However, aside from work, I have little joy. In the end, my wealth is only a fact of life that I am accustomed to. At this moment, lying on my bed and recalling my life, I realize that all the recognition and wealth that I took so much pride in have paled and become meaningless in the face of my death.
>
> You can employ someone to drive the car for you, make money for you, but you cannot have someone bear your sickness for you. Material things lost can be found or replaced. But there is one thing that can never be found when it's lost—Life. Whichever stage in life you are in right now, with time, you will face the day when the curtain comes down.
>
> Treasure love for your family, love for your spouse, love for your friends. Treat yourself well and cherish others. As we grow older, and hope-

fully wiser, we realize that a $300 or $30 watch both tell the same time. You will realize that your true inner happiness does not come from the material things of this world. Whether you fly first-class or economy, if the plane goes down— you go down with it.

Therefore, I hope you realize, when you have mates, old friends, brothers, and sisters whom you chat with, laugh with, talk with, have sung songs with, that is true happiness! Don't educate your children to be rich. Educate them to be happy so when they grow up they will know the value of things and not the price. Eat your food as your medicine; otherwise, you have to eat medicine as your food.

The One who loves you will never leave you ... even if there are 100 reasons to give up, he or she will find a reason to hold on to their friendship. There is a huge difference between a human being and being human. Only a few really understand it. You are loved when you are born. You will be loved when you die. In between, you have to manage!

The six best doctors in the world are sunlight, rest, exercise, diet, self-confidence and your friends!

Maintain them in all stages and enjoy a healthy life. (Steve Jobs)

When you reach that point, at the end of your life, what will your letter say? Perhaps some of the concepts outlined above can help in writing your story.

Relationships

It's a relationship business; we just happen to sell machines, engines and parts.

—Ron Choate, Caterpillar Inc.

On a well-designed flywheel, the bulk of the weight needs to be carried on the edges to maximize power generation. This is also true for effective leadership. When you put too much mass or emphasis in the center or at the top in a typical hierarchical organizational chart, you fail to leverage your entire organization.

The principle of relationships highlights that your ability to lead and inspire is dependent on connecting with employees at all levels of the organization and its extended value chain. This gets harder as you move up the organization, because you have to overcome the isolation and filters that exist between you and reality. If you do not think this is happening to you, think again. When I became a vice president at Caterpillar, I received a note from a colleague saying, "Welcome to the last day you will hear the truth." While there was a sarcastic tone to the note, it was a message I never forgot. While not easy, the best way to avoid this classic risk of leadership is to have meaningful relationships at all levels of the organization.

An effective leader thus must be able to build relationships not only to improve business results, but also for a much more rewarding personal journey. In interviews with a diverse group of 160 people from a variety of industries and roles, Rob Cross, co-author of the book *The Hidden Power of Social Networks*,[37] emphasizes that success in your career depends as much on your relationships—both connections at work and outside of work—as it does on your job itself. People whose work is mundane or demanding are as likely to feel satisfied and fulfilled as those with fun or inspiring jobs if they proactively invest in relationships that nourish them and create a sense of purpose.

Building relationships based on mutual trust and respect takes effort. The first and most important step is to let your employees know you care.

Show You Care

In the words of Theodore Roosevelt, "Nobody cares how much you know until they know how much you care."

You, as a leader, are responsible to build the culture within your teams. Research by Professor Kim Cameron[38] at the University of Michigan showed that workplaces characterized by caring, supportive, respectful, honest, and forgiving relationships demonstrated better organizational results. Likewise, Jane Dutton,[39] also at the University of Michigan and co-author of *Awakening Compassion at Work*, emphasized that compassion can foster greater workplace resilience.

In light of this, the only multiplier effect we have as leaders is capturing the hearts and minds of those we lead. This does not come from position, title, or an organizational chart; it comes from engaging with employees and, through that engagement, securing their trust and belief in us.

I had some great teachers along the way. Back in 2002, I came home from a business trip and was unpacking my suitcase when our daughter Ali came into our bedroom, sat on the bed, and talked to me while I unpacked. When I finished, I started to repack the suitcase for my next trip. Ali was upset and told me I could not leave again. I explained to her that the Caterpillar Chairman and CEO, Glen Barton, was flying to Geneva to pick me up and we were headed to Turkmenistan to meet with the president of the country. Ali said, "Well, okay, but just give Mr. Barton my warm regards."

After Glen and I spent a few days in Turkmenistan and were traveling back to Geneva, I opened my laptop, and my screensaver was a picture of my family. It reminded me of my conversation with Ali, and I told Glen the story and passed on Ali's warm regards. I went back to work on my laptop. A few minutes later, Glen handed me his business card with a personal note to Ali on the back.

Now, fast-forward to 2016. Sadly, after a long and courageous battle with cancer, Glen passed away. He meant a lot to me. We both came from small rural Missouri towns, and he served as a great mentor and example through the years. I sent a note to our kids giving them the sad news and, later that day, our daughter Ali stopped by with the card Glen had signed fourteen years previously with his personal message to her.

CATERPILLAR®

Glen Barton
Chairman and
Chief Executive Officer

Internet e-mail
barton_glen_a@cat.com

Caterpillar Inc.

100 N.E. Adams Street
Peoria, Illinois 61629
(309) 675-1331
Fax (309) 675-6171

His simple act of caring about me and my family not only helped shape me as a leader but also had an impact on a little girl who treasured the personal message. More than anything else, this simple, handwritten note on the back of a business card defined who Glen was. Yes, he was the Chairman and CEO of Caterpillar, but he was also a very special person who cared about the people he led, including their children. It was a lesson I never forgot.

As Glen's kind gesture demonstrates, building strong relationships is not about being a larger-than-life personality; it is about being humble and showing you care. In the words of Jim Collins,[40] "Level-5 leaders display a powerful mixture of personal humility and indomitable will. They are incredibly ambitious, but their ambition is first and foremost for the cause, for the organization and its purpose, not themselves." Every good-to-great transition in their research began with a level-5 leader who motivated the enterprise more with inspired standards than an inspiring personality. Through this sense of humility, you can build relationships that will yield strong results.

As leaders, we get opportunities to build these relationships through the thousand points of contact that we experience on our leadership journey. When I retired, I was amazed by the number of notes I received that started with "Once."

"Once, I picked you up at an airport."

"Once, I walked with you on the assembly line."

"Once, heading down to the cafeteria, I rode the escalator with you."

When you interact with employees, put away the cell phone, square your shoulders, look at them eyeball to eyeball, and listen. Ask them questions about where they grew up, their families and what are the things you do as a leader that make their job harder or easier. More importantly, remember these conversations and use them as opportunities to personally connect with them. No, you do not need to be superhuman in remembering all the details. Apps like Occasions can help your memory. Wish them a happy birthday or service anniversary. You will be surprised by the impact it will have.

As you engage, it will touch you as much as it matters to them. Once, I was traveling to a customer visit with someone in our organization that I had not met before, but time on the road always gives you an opportunity to get to know someone. During the conversation, we got on the topic of family, and he explained how he had lost his son who, while traveling in Vietnam on a scooter, had been hit by a car. When you hear a story like that, it cuts through to your core. Every year on the anniversary of his son's death, my note to this employee is simply, "You are in my thoughts and prayers." Because he is.

When you walk into a conference room with the senior people around the table and junior associates relegated to the back wall, do you ask everyone to make room for everybody at the table? When you walk into a crowded room full of your business colleagues, are you as interested in engaging with people at lower levels in the organization as you are with those at the top? As leaders, we get this opportunity every day, and while we may not remember the engagement, our employees will. We should never underestimate the power of our personal connections and having employees understand that we really do care.

The downside of building these relationships is that it makes tough decisions tougher. I will forever recall the 2009 global financial crisis and the need to restructure our workforce as sales went from $55 billion in 2008 to $32 billion in 2009. As we went through the list of people who had to be furloughed, in many cases I knew them personally. I remember coming home one evening worn out by the process. Ann asked me what was wrong, and I explained the difficulty of the process. However, it should be hard. If it is ever easy to make tough decisions like this, you have missed the plot. If you really do care, it will hurt. And that is okay.

Unpack Your Bags

You will never build strong and enduring relationships if the people you work with sense you are only passing through, more worried about the next job than doing the right thing in the right way in the current job. To build relationships founded on mutual trust and respect, you have to unpack your bags.

I vividly remember the first all-employee meeting when I took over a troubled division of Caterpillar located just outside Raleigh, North Carolina. In the Q&A session, a young lady at the front of the room asked a simple question: "Are you going to put down roots, or are you just passing through?" It was her way of asking, "Are you in this for personal advancement, or are you in it for the advancement of the division?" My response was that we had just moved into our house, our son was at a local university, and the ultimate answer to her question would be provided by my actions over time. Today, as we have settled in Raleigh, thinking about that question brings a smile to my face. We did put down deep roots.

We should all understand that the best way to get the next job is to do the current job exceptionally well. Early in my days of supervision, a young employee came into my office and said, "I want that job," every time a job was posted. My counseling on career advancement was always the same: It is a three-step process. First, give serious thought to what you want to do long-term, and a key determining factor is what you have a passion for. As I always told our children, find something you have a passion for and figure out how to turn it into a job, or you will work the rest of your life. Next, do an objective assessment of your current talents versus those required in the job you aspire to, and then find ways through personal development or on-the-job training to close that gap. And lastly, while completing steps one and two, always understand there is no substitute for strong performance on the current job.

This also applies to your personal life. When living in Geneva, Switzerland, and welcoming a new family who had transferred in from the U.S., I asked the spouse if she was excited about living in Geneva. Her response was, "It is a three-year assignment, and I can survive for three years." About six months later, at a wine tasting event, I ran into the couple again and asked how things were going. Her reply was, "We are six months in, and it's going fine." My response to her was, "Don't consider this a prison term." Make the most of the places you are in and the situations you experience.

Time and again, I saw people anxious to move on only to later regret not fully taking advantage of the opportunities presented along the way. In fact, one of my regrets is not fully immersing into the language and learning French when we lived in Geneva. When we were transferred to Geneva, I was told it would be a two- to three-year assignment; it ended up being nine years, and I took the easy way out. Life comes at us at a fast pace; without wishing time away, unpack your bags and make the most of the present.

Get Your Hands Dirty

We should all understand that engagement is a contact sport. When I took over responsibility for the Building Construction Products (BCP) Division, I realized that due to my lack of a manufacturing background, I would have to do something different to gain respect. I started a habit that lasted through my time as an officer of the company—working the assembly line one day a quarter. If you ever want to understand where your organization really stands, there is nothing like spending a day up close and personal with the people at all levels of the organization. Practices like this are also key to removing filters and isolation that typically exist between you and reality.

When I worked the assembly line, I worked the same station all day. It was the only way to get a real sense of how we were doing with standard work, safety, engagement, and more. While I worked the line in Clayton, North Carolina, in my early days at BCP, the conversation started with, "What are you doing here?" "Are you really going to have lunch with us?" "Are you staying all day?"

By the afternoon, the discussion changed to, "Where did you grow up?" "Do you have kids?" "Would you like to be part of our bowling team?"

At this point in BCP's history, we had a quality firestorm and had put a strategy in place to fix the problem. One day, at the end of a long shift, one of the guys on the assembly line pulled me aside and said, "Ed, I really do think you want to make a difference on quality, but you need to understand that the last three days of the month, the only thing people around here care about is getting the product out of the door."

The message was clear: Our strategy wasn't working. We did a complete reset, and while many things were involved in the turnaround of BCP, getting quality right was at the foundation. Doing it better started with getting my hands dirty. We revamped our quality strategy, and a key element was a "zone offense," dedicating resources to support the technicians on the line.

I continued this practice of working the assembly line until I retired. At my retirement gathering, there were a lot of kind gestures that touched me. But it was the presentation of a sculpture built by colleagues from the assembly line that meant the most to me. It is built from scrap, tells my career story, and is proudly displayed at my home in North Carolina.

While my experience was on the assembly line, you can apply the concept to any part of your business—riding with salespeople, spending a day with someone working supply-chain issues, etc. The importance is not with the job you select; it is in the direct engagement with employees at all levels of the organization. If you read about Sam Walton and how he built Walmart, you know he used this very principle, often showing up on third shift just to understand what was going on, and he always "left the entourage at home." The management layers between you and the people you engage with will always want to be involved; however, it stifles the openness of the discussion and sends the message that you really do not want to personally engage. I always kept the managers involved in the chain of command in the loop if key things developed from my engagement with employees, but I never needed the entourage.

Without a doubt, building strong and deep relationships requires time and effort. Unless you build it into your schedule, it will not happen. Perhaps the most important aspect of leadership is to simply show up. There was a poster as you entered the Executive Office of Caterpillar that said, "A desk is a dangerous place from which to see the world." Your only defense is a good offense, and that offense involves building opportunities to get your hands dirty so you can engage with employees at all levels of the organization.

Be Predictable

Our youngest daughter, Stef, is perhaps the most like me. We like the same music and read the same books. Often, I begin to say something and she finishes my sentence and then says, "Dad, you are so predictable." To which I always respond that predictability is a good trait in a father. It is also a good trait in a leader. Trust is a cornerstone of strong relationships, and being predictable is key to building this trust. It is hard to build trust if you are all over the map.

Now, this is not a predictability that is unresponsive to changing market conditions or competitive threats, but is based on the need for employees to understand how you think, establish priorities, and measure performance. If you run a large organization, you cannot be in all places at all times. Employees need a level of predictability that gives them the confidence to make decisions as they understand your direction, how you set priorities, and your expectations.

To get around the filters that exist in business, I used deep dives to directly engage with employees throughout the organization. I remember having a review with the medium-wheel loader team. At the end of the full-day review, they all had smiles on their faces, and I asked why. The leader of the group stood up and flipped over the flip chart. On it they had all the questions they anticipated that I would ask, and we had been through them all. It was this type of predictability I was always looking for—yes, in a deep dive and complete business review, but also in giving the organization the confidence to make decisions on their own. If you really want to empower your organization, give them a framework that clearly outlines expectations and then turn them loose.

Lastly, understand that predictability cuts two ways, both good and bad. A trusted colleague in the Caterpillar world tells the story of a product presentation where the team displayed a very detailed review of their plan, including things that had gone right and things that had gone wrong. The vice president in charge of the division railed on the team about the issues that had gone wrong. What he did not understand was that on future reviews, the negative news would be filtered out. The way we lead and the predictability associated with it will set the tone and the standard for what you do and do not get to see.

Simultaneous Lift

In today's competitive world, few businesses are vertically integrated. The vast majority of companies have suppliers as well as channel partners. Gone are the days when individual elements of the value chain can win in the long term at the expense of its other members. In fact, the future winners will be those who integrate across the value chain with relationships built on mutual trust and respect.

In the Caterpillar world, dealers are an incredible source of sustainable competitive advantage, and at the foundation are strong relationships. In 2006, we had a worldwide dealer meeting and, a week later, a worldwide supplier meeting. I remember going to the dealer meeting and feeling like I was going to my high school class reunion. I knew almost all the dealers worldwide, and in many cases, I knew their families as well. A week later, when I went to the worldwide supplier meeting, I felt like I was going to my wife's high school class reunion—no, we did not attend the same high school. I knew right then and there that was not right. We had great dealers, and yes, we had great suppliers as well. My general sense is that leaders do not fully embrace the extended value chain.

As I engaged with the Caterpillar value chain, including dealers and suppliers, the one thing that became obvious was that anytime performance was below par, improving it was always a simultaneous lift—we had to up our game in-house, and so did our dealers and suppliers. In my early days at BCP, we were struggling with product quality. At an all-employee meeting, one of the engineers stood up and said, "When are you going to fix the suppliers?" It was his assessment that our quality problems were solely related to the supply base. As a company, we had launched Six Sigma a number of years before this point in time, so for 30 days, we measured every quality excursion and then went back to find the root cause. What we found was that, in fact, our supply base needed to raise their game, but 50% of the quality excursions were due to internal defects related to Caterpillar—invasion of freeze periods, late engineering changes, inaccurate inventory records, and as mentioned earlier, the rush to get the product out of the door. The reality was, if we were going to improve quality, it needed to be a simultaneous lift.

This philosophy was also put to the test during the global financial crisis, when it would have been easy to look inward to protect our own business. Instead, we took an integrated value chain approach. For the first time in our history, to help dealers ease the burden on their balance sheets, we allowed them to cancel orders. In a very short period, in partnership with J. P. Morgan Chase, we launched a supplier finance program.

Understanding it was a simultaneous lift not only allowed us to get through the financial crisis when sales fell by more than 40% but also enabled us to respond quickly when market conditions improved. In the absence of meaningful relationships across the value chain, you run the risk of making mere commercial transactions. While that works in the short term, it certainly is not a long-term solution.

Lastly, as you embark on the simultaneous lift, always look for opportunities to do so at their place of business. I remember a product manager walking into my office in Geneva, Switzerland, and explaining how one of our dealers was not getting the job done. I asked him if he had been to the dealer's territory and ridden with salespeople and visited customers. His answer was, "No." My response was, "Go engage at their place of business and then we can have a meaningful discussion on where we go from here." As you know, in life there are always two sides to every story, and unless you engage with both, you will only get one side of the story.

Tying It All Together

Understand the only multiplier effect we have as leaders is capturing the hearts and minds of those we lead. This does not come from position, title, or an organizational chart; it comes from building strong relationships based on mutual trust and respect. As I came to learn, this applies in business as well as politics.

I had the good fortune of being transferred to Johannesburg, South Africa, in 1993, six months before the first free elections in that country. The leading candidate for the African National Congress was Nelson Mandela, who had spent 27 years in prison during the years of apartheid. He was a clear favorite to win the election as he had the unique ability to connect with and unite people from across the country.

Shortly after my arrival, the Caterpillar dealer in South Africa, Barlows, which was part of a large conglomerate, approached me about an aggressive marketing plan betting on a successful transition to a new government. Now, if you understand the plight of Africa, it was not a safe assumption at face value that all would be well. Just to the north of South Africa, Zimbabwe, prior to independence, had been the breadbasket of southern Africa with large exports of agricultural goods. Years after independence, they could not even feed their own nation.

As I probed about their level of confidence, the dealership told me about private meetings that were taking place with Nelson Mandela, the favored South African presidential candidate. For several months, Mandela had been meeting with key business leaders in South Africa. Through the years of apartheid, businesses were restricted on being able to take funds outside of the country, so they simply reinvested internally, creating large conglomerates. Five of these large companies made up a significant portion of South Africa's GDP, and Mandela was meeting with the CEOs of these companies privately, not only to get their counsel, but also to agree on a plan that would lead to a smooth transition. It was in these discussions that both the business leaders and Mandela built strong relationships grounded in mutual trust and respect.

Based on the relationship and trust built in these discussions, we put a plan in place to bet on a peaceful transition. We went on a road show, visiting every major area of the country, demonstrating our products, and talking about our confidence in the future of South Africa. We developed inventory and marketing plans that were launched around the time of the election. We realized significant gains in market share post election as our assumptions were right: it was a smooth and successful transition to a Mandela-led government.

The foundation for the planning of the transition was not born out of anger from 27 years in captivity or leveraged on a position of power leading the African National Congress party. It was built on strong relationships on the premise of mutual trust and respect between White business leaders and the future of a Black-majority-led government. President Mandela understood the power of strong relationships and leveraged them to ensure a smooth transition.

Operating Model

Execution is the ability to mesh strategy with reality, align people with goals, and achieve the promised results.

—Larry Bossidy, author and former CEO of AlliedSignal

Just as a flywheel transfers power from a motor to a machine, we transfer power to other people through how we live and lead. A flywheel only works when it is built according to its engineering drawing or blueprint. Your business needs a similar structure leading to clarity of direction.

To be clear, the flywheel is focused on an operating model that, by definition, is different from a business model. A business model describes how a business generates value. For example, at Caterpillar, we had four major business segments: mining, construction, energy, and a captive finance company. Across these, we focused on highly engineered products that, often involved a power train that transferred power from the engine to major components. We looked for products that had opportunity for selling parts and services as an offering. When the customer base was highly concentrated, we had a direct sales model. However, when the customer base was more dispersed, we worked with our global dealer organization, which is a significant competitive advantage. We felt products that aligned with these characteristics fit our business model and gave us the best opportunity to capture value.

While the business model describes how you generate value, an operating model drives execution and establishes a culture of how things get done. As leaders, you need a framework that constantly evaluates the external environment, selects priorities, and engages the entire organization to drive execution.

Historically, for many companies, the operating model has been something as simple as "management by objectives." If you lead people, you already have an operating model of some kind. It may be explicit with a very specific framework, or it may be implicit and something that you do, or your organization does, based on past practices or habits. However, in today's rapidly changing world, it needs to be more explicit, as remaining relevant is getting harder by the day.

According to a Credit Suisse report, disruptive forces are killing older companies much sooner than before. The average age of a registered company has fallen from almost 60 years in the 1950s to less than 20 years in current times. Making sure you and your company do not become one of these statistics requires an explicit operating model that allows you to not only adapt but also drive focused execution.

To drive value as a leader, you need a disciplined approach to provide your entire team with an unequivocal clarity of direction focused on the few things that will make the biggest difference.

My views on operating models have evolved over time based on my experiences as I came through the organization. I had the opportunity to participate in a Caterpillar process called the strategic planning committee that, upon a change in CEO, did a complete assessment of the external environment and challenged each and every aspect of how we were running the business. I had the benefit of some great leaders who taught me the discipline and rigor of Six Sigma and benefits of governance to create cadence and pace.

When I took over the Construction Industries segment of Caterpillar in late 2012 as a Group President residing in Singapore, I had two vice presidents located in the U.S., two in Europe, and two in Asia. Additionally, some teams had product responsibilities, while others were concerned with manufacturing and marketing. It quickly became apparent to the team that if we wanted to improve our business performance, we needed a common playbook or operating model. The model we developed incorporated the following five elements:

- A view from the outside in
- One definition of winning
- Granular Understanding Leading to Choice
- Cascade and cadence
- Culture and talent

A View from the Outside In

Today, the business landscape is challenging. Globalization, technology, and competition from all corners have made everyone's job far more complex. To overcome this challenge and remain relevant, your operating model needs an analysis of the changing market dynamics—trends affecting your company and customers, the talent pool, competition, how your customers make money, and more.

History has taught us it is not the biggest or strongest who survive; it is those who adapt based on external or competitive realities. Should we all not have seen the demise of malls when in our personal lives we were shopping at Amazon? Does Kodak regret inventing the digital camera but not bringing it to market in the hope of preserving their existing technology? Do the major auto companies wish they had gotten ahead of the shift to electric vehicles early on? At the end of 2021, Tesla's market cap was equal to the market cap of the next 10 most valuable global automakers combined.

I witnessed the power of an external assessment up close during my time at Caterpillar. More than 20 years ago, a small work group was formed to review changing external trends that would affect the industries we served. What they identified was the need to get into Compact Construction Equipment (CCE) to address two emerging trends. First, as labor availability was becoming scarce, they forecasted a shift from manual to mechanical labor (small excavators, instead of people digging trenches). Secondly, they projected the acceleration of urbanization, leading to the growth of machine applications working in tight spaces. Many leaders in the company pushed back on the expansion into the CCE product line as the division proposing the expansion was already struggling to make money and now wanted to expand into even smaller machines.

However, based on the strength of the external assessment and potential profitability, the plan was approved. Today, we have the benefit of hindsight. Over the past 20 years, the CCE industry has grown at a compounded annual growth rate of 13% and now represents almost 70% of the unit deliveries and half of the revenue of the entire division. It is not only a significant contributor to the Caterpillar product portfolio but has also provided opportunities for our dealers and suppliers.

Another key element of the external assessment is always doing a quality check on your sources of competitive advantage. At Caterpillar, we were blessed with two significant sources. The first was our dealer organization. Years ago, a *Wall Street* analyst estimated that Caterpillar dealers had twice the capital employed in the business as our next four largest competitors combined. I am very glad someone started building our dealer network back in 1925. Secondly, a big part of Caterpillar's secret sauce is systems integration—maximizing the performance of machine systems that get the most out of our engines, transmissions, hydraulic systems, and more. You should regularly review your sources of competitive advantage to make sure they are still relevant.

While I made mistakes along the way, the more I came to understand the operating model, the more it led to better business decisions, especially in relation to growth opportunities. As the team assessed new opportunities, we ran them through a more rigorous filter:

- Did the opportunity play to the strengths of our business model?
- Did we have sources of sustainable competitive advantage?
- Were customers who served the target industry profitable?

It is far easier to make money in an industry where your customers make money. Too often, growth initiatives or acquisitions are justified by line-item forecasted improvements in a spreadsheet instead of stepping back and looking at the broader issues first—issues such as does the size of the market make it worth pursuing, are competitors currently serving the opportunity profitable, and do you have sources of real and sustainable competitive advantage?

An external assessment does not only work in the business community but also functions well in the world of ALS research. The harsh reality of the disease is that while it has been studied since the mid-1800s, an ALS diagnosis is still considered a death sentence, as no one knows the cause or has a cure. Out of the last 200 ALS drug trials, only two drugs have been approved that have marginally affected life expectancy by fewer than 12 months. The external world has changed, and some visionary neurologists supported by business leaders have seen the opportunity to harness the power of the exponential changes in the world of technology to solve what those who have gone before us have failed to do. Something had to change, and Answer ALS was born out of the external assessment of the world around us.

Instead of having theories about pathways and proceeding with expensive drug trials, the team took a step back, understood how technology had evolved, and decided to come at the disease from a different perspective. They asked the question, "How do we drive collaboration using an open-source platform of big data, machine learning, and artificial intelligence to uncover the mysteries of ALS?" Today, Answer ALS is using these capabilities to make a difference— open collaboration between 24 research centers and eight clinical institutions, collecting six billion data points on each of the 1000 patients and 200 controls—all loaded onto one portal with open access to anyone in the world doing ALS research.

If you look at the pandemic, that, too, has highlighted not only the importance of this external assessment but also how one can win even during tough times. Yes, the pandemic brought many businesses to their knees, but others have seized the opportunity and taken advantage of the shift to online, home delivery, and more. The pandemic has taken external trends that were already in play and accelerated them. Even when travel returns, many former face-to-face meetings will remain online. Post-pandemic, businesses will rethink their work-from-home models and assess if they have more office capacity and cost than they need. My mother never ordered groceries online, but going forward, even post-pandemic, it is a habit she will probably maintain. As the old saying goes, "Never waste a good crisis." A good external assessment is key to taking full advantage.

As you do your external assessment, some of the questions you should ask are set out below:

- What are your sources of competitive advantage, and are they still relevant?
- Are the markets you serve profitable for customers as well as others that serve the industry?
- Are there new and emerging competitors entering the market?
- Are there broader societal shifts that can affect your business?
- Are there political, trade, or pending tax changes that will affect your business?
- Are there opportunities in new growth areas or adjacent spaces where you have sources of competitive advantage from which your operating model can extract value?

In other words, conduct an examination of the political, economic, social, and technological landscape of the external environment, otherwise known as a PEST analysis.

Though a formal external assessment should be repeated annually, you need your eyes open to emerging trends. As the pandemic illustrated, life does not always conform to a calendar-year approach to planning. While the timing may vary based on circumstances, one thing that does not change is the need for a clear understanding of the external environment and what it can do. If there is one part of the model where you may need to leverage an external resource, this is it. Sometimes, within the organization, we are simply too myopic to see larger shifts or competitive threats.

One Definition of Winning

If you go to any type of sporting event around the world, when you come to the end, there is always a clear indication of the winner—the scoreboard says it all. In American football, time of possession, offensive yards gained, defensive yards allowed, and turnovers all matter, but the ultimate definition of winning is the final score. At times in the business world, we make it too complex and become overly enamored with a multitude of metrics. And while metrics can give you indicators of the health of the business, at the end of the day (or game), you need one clear definition of winning.

In any business, it all starts with winning through the eyes of your customers. At Caterpillar, we were focused on customers making more money with our products, services, and solutions than they could with our competitors. However, doing this without capturing a share of the value for shareholders would be a shallow victory as we would not have the funds to reinvest in the business. Through trial and error during my career, I became a strong advocate of a definition of winning based on economic profit. *Economic profit* is the earnings generated by a company or business minus a charge for the capital employed to generate those earnings. Measures such as operating profit after capital charge (OPACC), return on capital employed (ROCE), or economic value added (EVA) provide that information.

Although they are different terms, all these measure profit and take into consideration the cost of assets required to generate that profit.

A measure of economic profit should be the definition of winning for two key reasons: First, over the long haul, it is how the market will reward you. In my days as the Caterpillar CFO, it became apparent that the models used by financial analysts were trying to estimate the future stream of cash flow and then discounting it back to current value as an assessment of value. Secondly, to remain relevant over the long haul, you need a reinvestment advantage against your key competitors. To the degree that you can gain a higher share of the economic profit than your competitors, you have a tremendous competitive advantage. Let us take a look at a real-world example.

In the early days of the mobile device movement, the market assessed whether the winner would be Apple or Samsung. Early on, some pointed to the higher share of handset volume secured by Samsung and failed to see that while Apple's share of unit volume was lower, they dominated with their share of economic profit. They took the benefits of this higher share of profits and reinvested in the business, including upgrades to the iPhone. They launched new products, such as AirPods and the Apple Watch, and expanded their services platform. To this day, they continue to dominate in the share of economic profit. Not least, their shareholders have also been appropriately rewarded.

Without the right definition of winning, your organization can declare success but fail to position the business for the future. Caterpillar has been historically known for our medium and large machines. When we expanded into the highly competitive small-machine segment, we struggled to make money, as in many cases we had a large- and medium-machine approach to the business. Over time, we seemed to accept the underperformance of the division and adopted a definition of winning based on the division being the "strategic underbelly." The thought was that if we competed in small machines (the underbelly), we could prevent small-machine competitors from growing into our more traditional product lines. However, for many, "strategic underbelly" translated into being okay to lose money as long as we kept small-machine competitors from growing into our more traditional product lines.

This was not a sustainable definition of winning, as it did not provide funding for future products or manufacturing investment. As the company went through its resource allocation process, this segment always came up short because it was not profitable. As a team, we first recentered our focus on profitability, then went through the journey to break even, and then from breaking even to generating economic profit. Upon reflection, a mistake I made was not taking the time to explain the "why" on the need for economic profit. Without this explanation, employees throughout the organization assumed we were trying to satisfy Wall Street.

For many in the organization, this was not the best motivator. The reason economic profit matters is that, without it, you cannot secure a reinvestment advantage versus your competition. With it, you can invest in the business, which not only fuels growth for the company but also creates opportunities for employees in the form of advancement, compensation, and a sense of being part of a winning team. If you communicate the "why," you can develop an "owner's mentality" throughout your employee base.

The single definition of winning advantage also applies in the world of neurology. Yes, Answer ALS is an incredibly complex project involving 1000 patients, 200 controls, six billion data points per patient, IPS cells, motor neurons, and multiomics, but there is only one definition of winning—discovering the subgroups that make up the disease. Similar to that of cancer, our hypothesis is that there is not one form of ALS but multiple subgroups. Until those groups are identified, we believe any drug trial is a bit of a shot in the dark, as demonstrated by past failed drug trials.

As you think about the right definition of winning for your organization, avoid the tendency to have it be activity based: number of customers, annual sales or shipments, inventory turns, or just a market share measurement. It needs to be a clear, profit-oriented economic metric that matters to the future of the business. Yes, there are leading indicators, but in my days as a CFO, I never had a single investor give us credit for activities per share.

Granular Understanding Leading to Choice

A core element of the operating model is the belief that in every business, there is a high concentration of where value is created and destroyed. In the vast majority of companies, less than 50% of the capital deployed generates the vast majority of their profitability. Conversely, significant chunks of capital deployed actually destroy shareholder value. As a leader, to drive value, you need a disciplined approach to acknowledge this reality and provide clarity of direction focused on where you want to grow or fix your business.

In the book *Beliefs, Behaviors, & Results*, authors Scott Gillis and Joe Shalleck[41] highlight that you can pick any industry and you will see economic profit concentration by company within the industry, pick any company and you will see economic profit concentration by business across the corporate portfolio, and pick any business and you will see economic profit concentration by product/channel/ region and customer segment. Do not think for a minute that your business is an exception.

As you move up the organization, the tendency will always be to manage the business through averages, to manage total profitability by a product line or geographic territory. When you manage the business at a high level and through averages, it is difficult to drive improvement in profitability above the rate of change in the industries you serve. Opportunities to drive business performance do not lie in the averages. The truth lies in a granular understanding of where you create (make money) and destroy (lose money) value in the business.

Assuming you pick the right definition of winning focused on economic profit, understand there is a big difference between "measuring" economic profit and "managing" it. Some companies have launched efforts to measure economic profit, link it to incentive compensation, and then call it a day. It takes much more. It has to be the way you look at the business, manage the business, and allocate resources. A huge part of this effort is having a granular understanding of the business.

When I first became part of the Caterpillar Construction Industries team, I was a bit overwhelmed with the size and complexity of the division. We sold product in virtually every country in the world, our products ranged from trucks that could haul 85 tons in a single payload to mini excavators that weighed one ton. Our manufacturing facilities spanned the world, including the United States, Latin America, Europe, and Asia. However, through a granular understanding of the business, it became apparent that, in each part of the organization, there were no more than a handful of initiatives that, if executed successfully, could play a major role in improving the division's performance. When business seems complex, a granular understanding can simplify matters and shine light on the few things that really matter.

Doing this right, of course, starts with the correct definition of winning. This clarity then allows you to evaluate success or profitability by product, by market, and by geographic area. Now, getting to this detail is a heavy lift, but you need to understand your profitability by product, by market, and by customer. Some will tell you to shy away from this approach because you have to allocate certain costs to assess profitability. But the benefits far outweigh the disadvantages. When you have this clarity, it opens your eyes to the greatest opportunities to grow the most profitable parts of the business and how to address those destroying shareholder value. You unleash the creative and competitive spirit that lies in those you lead. Everybody wants to be part of a winning effort—be it to grow a strong part of your business or to turn around a weak one.

As a leader, avoid the trap of assuming you can now fly at 30,000 feet. Yes, you need a broad understanding of the overall business, but get your hands dirty, secure a granular understanding of the business, and then make choices—allocating resources to those few things that are going to make the biggest difference. Think of it as being your own internal "activist." Stay ahead of the external world by constantly evaluating your own portfolio and clearly understanding where you create and destroy value. Then appropriately allocate resources to achieve results.

Cascade and Cadence

As you move up the corporate ladder, you will come to understand that your success is not based on your individual capability but instead on your ability to manage, motivate, and lead people. The multiplier effect is realized when everyone in your organization understands their role. One leader I learned a lot from was Giancarlo Bertoluzzo, the CEO of the Caterpillar dealership in northern Italy. He was a very clear thinker and could get his entire organization focused on the few things that mattered the most. He shared a story about the importance of cascading vision down the organization.

He told about a quarry owner in the Carrara marble region of Italy. Carrara marble is a type of white or blue-gray marble quarried in the city of Carrara, located in the province of Massa and Carrara in the Lunigiana, the northernmost tip of modern-day Tuscany, Italy. One day the quarry owner walked into the quarry, saw a young man, and asked him, "What is your job?" to which the young man replied, "I just shape stones from the time I come into work to the time I go home."

That evening, as the quarry owner thought about the young man's answer, he felt uncomfortable with his view of his job. So the next day, the quarry owner took the young man into the village where a great cathedral was being built, and he showed the young man where in the church his stones were being placed. The next day, the owner went to the quarry, saw the young man, and asked him what he did, to which the young man replied, "I build great cathedrals."

As leaders, our job is to help every employee understand where their stones are being placed as we work toward our vision. Never underestimate an employee's ability or desire to understand the role they play. Simply by cascading that understanding down the organization, you will be amazed by what can be achieved.

A key element of the cascade is establishing cadence—governance and execution at a pace. Very few organizational designs have all required resources in one part of the organization. Matrix organizations are a reality, and trust me, there is no such thing as a perfect organizational chart. The more matrixed the organization, the greater the requirement for focus and cadence.

Typically, the cascade begins from the top and is driven down the organizational hierarchy. Leaders at every level then translate and align that to their own functional areas. This is a critical step during normal times, but perhaps even more critical during a time of crisis. While for many the global financial crisis is a distant memory, for me it is forever clearly etched in my memory. As mentioned previously, at Caterpillar, we went from $55 billion in sales in 2008 to $32 billion in sales in 2009. In a capital-intensive industry, that is a downshift to the tenth degree. However, as a team, we pulled together and kept the business in the black, maintained the dividend, and protected our credit rating—the "hat trick," as we called it—safeguarding the viability of the company.

I was then a member of the Executive Office of Caterpillar, with responsibility for the finance side of the house. My part of the team was focused on proactively managing balance sheet liquidity throughout the entire supply chain and communicating with investors and rating agencies. We agreed on the definition of winning and identified the key work streams. Key objectives and targets were cascaded throughout that tied to the "hat trick." On cadence, core cross-functional team meetings were held every Wednesday, and executive stakeholder meetings were conducted every Friday at 7:00 a.m. The agenda was straightforward and consistent: What did you get done this week? What will you get done next week? And what decisions do you need from the Executive Office to keep things on track? This created a cadence and sense of urgency that kept the team focused and engaged. While I take great pride in many aspects of my Caterpillar career, it was how the team navigated 2009 that brings me the greatest sense of accomplishment.

These same principles also apply in my world of ALS research. Shortly after the Answer ALS project was launched, the lead neurologist approached me about the possibility of taking over a leadership position on the advisory board. As I thought about it, I explained to him that this is how I work: We will have a single definition of *winning*, we will focus our efforts on the work streams that matter most, and we will cascade this focus down the organization and establish a cadence to drive execution. After I outlined my approach, I asked him, "Are you sure you want me involved?" His response was, "It's not what I want, but it's what we need." We have brought the basic principles of an operating model to the world of neurology research, and I remain hopeful that we will make a difference in what is a tough disease.

If you want to deliver strong results, cascade the elements of the operating model and areas of focus throughout the organization in a way that all understand the roles they play, with a clear definition of winning. I remain convinced that 99.9% of employees walk through the door each day wanting to do the right thing in the right way. If they are not doing what they should be doing, the first place to look for correction is yourself. Have you provided the clarity of direction and then cascaded it through your organization in a way that each employee understands the role they play?

Culture and Talent

The last and perhaps the most critical element of an operating model is culture and talent. I subscribe to Peter Drucker's belief that "Culture eats strategy for breakfast." To be clear, he did not mean that strategy is not important; rather, that an empowering culture is a surer route to organizational success than a mere strategy.

As a common definition, *culture* is defined by the organization's unwritten rules, rituals and practices. It is what we do unconsciously. Bill Taylor, the author of *Simply Brilliant: How Great Organizations Do Ordinary Things in Extraordinary Ways*,[42] shared his learning about the culture at Amazon. Jeff Bezos insisted for years that desks in the office be built by buying cheap doors from Home Depot and nailing legs to them. Even though they could pay for elegant desks, the idea was to remind everyone that "we look for every opportunity to save money so we can deliver the best products for the lowest cost." This is what culture is: setting the rules of the game and leading by example each and every day.

When developing and deploying an operating model to deliver results, avoid the tendency to make it merely a mechanical process of walking through the steps or being fixated on the accounting or profit target, because it is more about the culture than it is about accounting. Results come when your people understand how you look at the business, how you establish priorities, and how you measure success. I always believed, if I was traveling somewhere in Latin America or another part of the world and not available, and employees in India or China had to make decisions, based on the disciplined framework and clarity of direction provided, they would know how I would think and what decisions I would make.

The desired culture is heavily influenced by the people you put on your team. We all know how time-consuming and disruptive picking the wrong person for your team is versus how easy it is when you have the right talent running the business. I am a huge believer in sports analogies, and I think there are two that directly apply to people. First, the general manager of a baseball team never delegates draft day. In many instances, we delegate key hiring decisions to others in the organization. Yes, HR can run the process, but I wanted leaders on my team involved in selecting people who desired balance, built relationships, and had the discipline to deliver results.

Secondly, I grew up a St. Louis Cardinals baseball fan and always appreciated the rivalry they had with the Chicago Cubs. I enjoyed the fact that the Cardinals had won 11 World Series, and the Cubs none. However, that changed in 2016, after the Cubs finally figured out that the way to build a great team is through a strong farm system—growing the team from within. Yes, from time to time you may need to go outside to hire a specific talent, but your primary focus should be on developing and promoting talent from within. Understand that when you have to go outside for talent, it could be an indication of the failure of your own people development model.

In selecting people for my team, the three key attributes at the top of my list were "collaborative, disciplined, and self-aware."

- *Collaborative.* Leaders who collaborate are more focused on the enterprise, whereas those that do not, are more worried about their personal advancement. Politics is a real issue in any company, and I always wanted to understand who was running for office versus who was running the business.

It is hard to envision an organization that does not have elements of a matrix. At Caterpillar, one division made components, another designed machines, another was responsible for manufacturing and supply chain, and we dealt with a global network of suppliers and dealers. If you wanted to make great progress on the few initiatives that mattered most, it always involved collaboration across organizational chart boundaries. During my time at Caterpillar, I worked in several different organizational structures, and one thing is apparent—there is no such thing as a perfect organizational chart. Often, leaders try to resolve issues of collaboration through changing the organizational chart. A more productive way is to make sure you have the right culture, with everyone following the same operating model.

- *Disciplined.* A cornerstone of the operating model is discipline—discipline in adhering to the single definition of *winning*, in selecting and sticking to the few things that matter most, in driving a governance process with structure and cadence. Therefore, to be successful, pick leaders who have the required discipline in how they lead.

I had the benefit of working for leaders early in my career who taught me a lot about rigor and discipline. I was part of the team that set global production schedules for Caterpillar facilities. We had to present our recommendations to a division manager who was known for his tough questions focused on the details. I came to understand he was not doing it to be hard on us; he was doing it to get a sense for the rigor and discipline we were bringing to the job. It was a lesson I have never forgotten. I think in today's world, a lack of discipline in the way we lead is a huge gap and one that cannot prevail if you want to succeed.

- *Self-aware.* The third key attribute is the largely underappreciated leadership quality of self-awareness, because the flywheel requires leaders who connect with their people. You need leaders who know if their employees understand what they are trying to achieve, who know when they are connecting with their people and, more importantly, when they are not. As I observed leaders engaging with their people, I was always looking for signs of this self-awareness.

  I remember traveling in Europe with a colleague. While we were waiting at the airport for our flight, the individual expressed his interest in moving up the organization and leading people. A few minutes later, our flight was delayed, and he promptly went to the ticket counter, chastised the attendant, and demanded to understand the reason for the delay. I remember observing all this and thinking, was he really oblivious to the fact that I was observing this behavior and understanding that it was an indication of his leadership style and capability? His lack of self-awareness was a heads-up to me that he was not the right fit for my organization.

  Always thoroughly observe the people in your organization, from the way they treat and lead their people to the way they treat a waiter, Uber driver, or person behind the counter when a flight is delayed. It speaks volumes about the type of leaders they are.

Finally, there is one more last and difficult step related to the operating model—you have to put your approach down in writing. Writing ensures you are crystal clear with your intent and direction. If you give me any set of PowerPoint slides, I can give you five different presentations by varying tone and points of emphasis. Reportedly, any proposal that comes to Jeff Bezos, the former CEO of Amazon, has to be in writing to ensure clarity. When you put it in writing as a narrative, your intent and direction become crystal clear.

Importantly, too, use language the entire organization can understand. One time, our former Chairman and CEO, Jim Owens, was speaking to a large audience at North Carolina State University about the global economy and U.S. competitiveness. At a dinner with local dignitaries that evening, one of the participants said, "What I liked about your presentation was that you talked about very complex global issues but you used 'Walmart English'—I understood every word you said."

Business is relatively simple; unfortunately, we have the tendency to make it complex. Keep the words describing your disciplined approach to delivering results simple and straightforward and cascade them throughout all levels of your organization. I remember being at an all-employee meeting in Wuxi, China, and in the Q&A, one of our young China leaders asked the question, "On page 8, you said…is that really what you meant?" His question put a smile on my face, and my response was, "Yes, and I so appreciate your effort to understand the model."

Tying It All Together

A number of the examples used throughout the book tie back to my time at the Building Construction Products Division (BCP). In 2004, I was assigned to the division, and it had struggled for years. Caterpillar was built on the backs of medium and large machines serving heavy construction, mining, and other industries. BCP was a relatively new division that built much smaller machines serving nontraditional markets, such as light construction and landscaping. Over its 20+ year history, it had lost money the majority of the time. My assignment was clear: figure out if we should/could reverse this trend or exit the business.

As we assessed the external markets and opportunity, it became clear there was a significant and growing market. The world's population was urbanizing, leading to the need for small machines that could work in confined spaces. Another key trend was the move from manual to mechanical labor. It was getting harder to find people to dig trenches, do landscaping, or do other forms of manual work, leading to an opportunity for machines as a replacement. Lastly, competitors that served these markets made good money. In our case, it was more likely a case of poor execution than being in the wrong market, as our competitors were making attractive returns in the same market. We compared our performance to that of our competitors and saw huge opportunities for improved performance in areas such as quality, product cost, and more.

We then focused on our definition of winning. As covered above, the focus on winning (profitability) evolved over time. It started with getting the business to break even. After that objective was achieved, the focus shifted to operating profit after capital charge, which would lead to reinvestment opportunities.

The team gained a granular understanding of the business. Yes, it was a complex business with multiple product lines and facilities located around the world, sourcing components from a vast supplier network and selling to dealers in virtually every country of the globe. However, through a granular understanding of the business, we chose to focus on five strategic initiatives that could erase the vast majority of the loss, cascaded the focus down through the organization, and set a cadence to drive execution. For example, one area of focus was quality. On the challenged product lines, we had weekly meetings that always concluded with who was going to do what and by when. It did not take people long to understand that coming to those meetings without completing the assigned work was simply not an option. It drove a pace and sense of urgency that we desperately needed.

While it took time and the movement of some leaders who simply did not want to get on board, slowly but surely, the culture started to shift. In the early days, BCP was a division that most people within the Caterpillar organization wanted to stay away from, as it was a troubled one. However, through time and results, it became a place that many wanted to call home based on the culture that existed.

Perhaps the best part of the BCP story is that my replacement and her team took the division to even higher levels, which is the ultimate measure of leadership—leaving the business better than you found it and in more capable hands. She even went as far as having a ceremonial burial of the concept of "strategic underbelly" in a box at one of the facilities. It was a clear statement: we were not going back. Even today, I sometimes hear people say, "BCP was your favorite." My response remains the same: "You deliver the same type of results and you'll be my favorite as well."

In many ways, driving an operating model leading to results is like the story of Sisyphus in Greek mythology, to whom Zeus dealt the eternal punishment of forever rolling a boulder up a hill. Every time the boulder reached the peak, it rolled back down the hill and Sisyphus had to start all over. Leadership is not punishment, but it is also not for the faint of heart. A reality of leadership is that you deliver great results and the next year you get to do it all over again.

You need a disciplined approach to assist you in the effort of once again pushing the boulder up the hill. You have to be aware of the external environment, set a clear definition of winning, gain a granular understanding of the business, and choose to focus on the few things that are going to make the biggest difference. You cascade it down the organization and drive a cadence and pace that creates a sense of urgency. And you select and develop leaders who buy into the model and set the example, leading to a culture of winning in the right way. You keep doing it over and over to build a great business.

There is no doubt that the approach you take will vary depending on the kind and size of organization you lead or the clarity you get from your superiors. But I believe it works, whether you lead five or 50,000 employees. It works in guiding an organization or executing a complex project.

Discipline Leading to Habits

*We are what we repeatedly do. Excellence, then, is
not an act but a habit.*

—Will Durant

The principles outlined earlier in this book, for the most part,
are just good old common sense. To live and lead a good life, you
need to have balance, build strong relationships, and provide your
organization clarity of direction. If the principles are straightforward,
why is it so difficult? I would offer that a higher level of personal discipline is required, and when consistently executed, it morphs into
habits or new ways of doing things.

The challenge associated with introducing change is thrust
upon us at the beginning of each year. According to the US News

& World Report,[43] up to 80% of all New Year's resolutions fail by the second week of February. Now, this is not because people do not want to change. Rather, the root cause of failure is not deploying a systematic approach to forming new habits that lead to the desired change.

As an ancient Chinese philosopher and writer, Lao Tzu, points out, this can be good or bad.

> Watch your thoughts; they become your words.
> Watch your words; they become your actions.
> Watch your actions; they become your habits.
> Watch your habits; they become your character.
> Watch your character; it becomes your destiny.

Let us start with a basic understanding of how the mind works.

Workings of the Mind

In creating change—whether it relates to diet, exercise, or something else—I remain amazed at how little the workings of the mind come into the discussion. It is the most powerful tool we have at our disposal. As you can see from the next page, the conscious mind is a small portion of the critical mind. Its role is to take in information and analyze it to determine whether some action should be taken or not. It is always making a decision that is either a yes or a no. Whenever it says yes to a piece of incoming information, the subconscious accepts it and reacts instantaneously. And when it is a no, the subconscious refuses to accept it and lets the stimuli pass. Both these functions of acceptance and rejection occur at the conscious level. Some examples of conscious decision-making are stopping at a red light, deciding what we are going to eat for breakfast, driving from point A to point B, or buying a birthday present. These are very deliberate conscious processes.

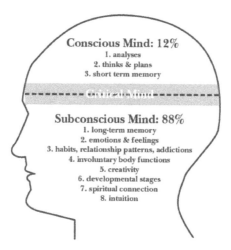

Theory of Mind by Dr. Kappas
(simplified)

The subconscious mind, on the other hand, processes information automatically so you do not have to think about things you do. It is what keeps you the way you are. The way this happens is that it behaves as a massive underground mental library that permanently stores all your memories, habits, behaviors, deep-seated emotions—really, everything that you have learned and experienced up to this point in life. Left unstimulated, it self-regulates you like a thermostat to act in accordance with who you are. Its role is to make sure that you always think, behave, and perform in a manner consistent with the information you have accepted as true in the conscious mind. One example of the subconscious in action is breathing—we do not have to think at all to breathe, but if we do concentrate on it, we can change how we control our breathing patterns. Other examples include typing on a keyboard without looking—it starts as a learned skill requiring concentration, but through repetition, it becomes automatic. When brushing your teeth, you do not consider whether to use your right or left hand; it happens automatically.

Psychologist Sigmund Freud often used the metaphor of an iceberg to describe these two levels of the mind. The tip of the iceberg that extends above the water represents the conscious mind. Beneath the water is the much larger bulk of the iceberg, which represents the subconscious. While the conscious mind is important, Freud believed it was far less vital than the subconscious. The things that are hidden from awareness, he believed, exert the greatest influence over our personalities and behaviors.

In the normal course of life, you pick up new experiences at the conscious level and, over time, relegate them to your underground mental library (the subconscious). To enable a change or develop a new habit, you will have to first exercise your conscious mind, which, over time and only with repeated practice, will relegate that new behavior to the subconscious mind, thereby putting it on an auto mode and becoming a new habit.

As an illustration, imagine you want to change something about yourself. Maybe you decide it is time to get into better shape. In your conscious mind, you know that is a good idea. You will be healthier, feel better, look better, and maybe even live longer. Yet at every step of the journey, things do not go the way you want them to. You cannot seem to make it to the gym, and you keep finding yourself with a cookie in your hand, cheating on your diet, even though you know better.

Clearly, it is not enough for the 12% (conscious) to want to change, as the 88% (subconscious) will win every time. To the subconscious, the gym is a foreign concept and not part of the regular routine. It is an unknown. Left to its own, it would rather stick with the status quo and relegate your actions to those you are familiar with rather than take a risk with an unknown. As for the diet, those cookies have definite positive associations in the subconscious, and it may be responding to parts of the body that crave sugar. It is going to want more and more.

Under these conditions, the subconscious by design is slow to change. How many people do you know who say, "I want to stop smoking" or "I want to spend more time with my family," but it never happens? The pull of the subconscious is strong, and it will take you back to who you currently are as soon as it can, unless the vision of who you want to be is stronger and more compelling.

But what if you could get past the critical "firewall" of your mind and insert a few positive associations in place of the negatives and unknowns you have about losing weight, going to the gym, or carving out time for the family?

This is where the critical mind comes into the picture. It kicks in when you have a conflict or tension. The term for this is *cognitive dissonance,* and it is described as feelings of discomfort that result when your beliefs run counter to your behavior and/or new information that is presented to you. For the critical mind to do its work, you have to create a conflict between who your subconscious relegates you to be and who you want to be. For example, if at the subconscious level you are used to sleeping in until 6:30, grabbing a shower and a cup of coffee, and then heading off to work, wanting to insert exercise into your morning routine will not happen until you have an alternative vision for the morning that specifically details your new desired behavior—wanting to get up at 5:30, exercise for 45 minutes, followed by coffee, a well-balanced breakfast, and then heading off to work.

In principle, to grow or change, you have to create conflict, a problem, or a burning platform. This is where most will say all the suggestions make sense but it is just too hard to change. Only you can decide if it is worth the effort, but if your answer is yes, it is a fairly straightforward four-step process:

- Goal setting and action plans
- Affirmations
- Daily prescription
- Accountability

The process starts by beginning with the end and the goals you want to achieve in mind.

Goal Setting and Action Plans

A line from songwriter George Harrison's "Any Road"—"If you don't know where you're going, any road will take you there"—is quite apt here. In many ways, based on the way the mind works, this is the road many of us are on. We become products of the environment in which we have grown up, and we go through the motions year after year. Now, in some cases, this could be a really good thing, based on one's surroundings, but remember, you also have the ability to chart your own course and deliver better results. While the vision you set earlier provides a high-level aspirational direction, here you establish more specific goals and actions focused on improving the way you live and lead. In the absence of goals and action plans, your vision merely gathers dust on the shelf and you continue to meander through life in a reactive mode.

A key part of goal setting is that you need to have clarity on exactly what you want to change. Just thinking about your goals or having an idea at a high level is not enough. More importantly, setting goals only works if you write them out. A study by psychology professors Sarah Gardner and Dave Albee[44] at Dominican University, in California, in a sample of 149 participants, found that those who wrote their goals accomplished significantly more than those who did not.

As you write them out, make them SMART—specific, measurable, actionable, relevant, and time bound. Doing so will keep you in check. The more specific you are about your goals, the more likely you will be able to accomplish them. This means that you do not just say you want to make more money or lose more weight; you have to say exactly how much money you want to make or how much weight you want to lose. You have to put real and exact figures on them, and they need to be realistic and attainable. For example, losing 50 pounds in the first month may be impossible, and certainly, not healthy. Based on your schedule and your past attempts, be realistic. Maybe losing five pounds in the first month is more practical on the way to the long-term goal of losing 50 pounds. The idea is to not overwhelm yourself but to stay motivated and build momentum toward your ultimate goal.

Next, make those goals measurable so you can track your progress and stay motivated. Assessing progress helps you to stay focused and it gives you the excitement of getting closer to realizing your goal. As an example, you can measure your goal of getting to your desirable weight (to lose 25 pounds) by determining what you have to do (exercise five days a week) to attain the goal within six months' time.

The third step in goal setting is to take action. For example, through the years my goals have varied at home and work. One of my personal goals was to be at my target weight of 170 pounds, with a 34-inch waist. To achieve this, my action items were to work out for 45 minutes a minimum of five days a week and weigh every Monday and Friday. When weighing on Friday, if I was at my target weight, I would relax a bit over the weekend, but if I was above the target, I would remain disciplined and watch my diet. Your goals will not be realized by merely writing them down; they have to be aligned with specific actions and be measurable.

The fourth step is about ensuring that your goals are relevant and align with your burning platform. Is your goal worthwhile? Is this the right time to get started? The fifth and last step is to ensure that they are time-bound. You have to set an exact date by when you plan to achieve your goals. Focus on goals that are in shorter intervals. If you plan to achieve a 50-pound weight loss in one year, then break that down into three-month intervals. That is 12.5 pounds every three months.

Once you have your goals and action plans in place, you are ready for the next powerful part of the process.

Affirmations

While goals and action items point you in the right direction, affirmations enable the change. The dictionary defines *affirmations* as "statements or propositions that are declared to be true." They are positive statements that relate to a goal, desirable situation, or state of being, and they are repeated frequently.

According to research, everything that we repeatedly say to ourselves, out loud or in our thoughts, is an affirmation. The reticular activating system (RAS) is a part of our brain that makes words that get repeated over time a part of our identity, regardless of whether they are positive or negative. On the positive side, if a parent or teacher tells children over and over that they can achieve anything, they set their minds to it and that becomes a part of who they are. Sadly, the reverse is true as well. If children are told over and over that they are not good enough or not cut out for school, they will soon come to believe it. The same logic applies across other situations. What you tell yourself or believe in is what you become. Remember, your thoughts become words, actions, and, eventually your character and destiny.

Research shows that when affirmed, you are more likely to take the first steps toward positive behavioral change. A study by Peter Harris, Kathryn Mayle, Luch Mabbott, and Lucy Napper[45] at the University of Sheffield, England, showed how affirmations increased openness to information about the dangers of smoking. They presented smokers with graphic antismoking cigarette advertisements. Relative to participants in a control condition, participants who self-affirmed, listing their desirable qualities, saw the advertisements as more distressing, expressed greater confidence in their abilities to stop smoking, and had a stronger motivation to quit. Similarly, in another study, Christopher Armitage[46] from the University of Manchester found that among the affirmed participants, 59% took leaflets about how to quit smoking, compared with only 37% of non-affirmed participants. In conclusion, affirmations take you closer to achieving your goals.

The value of affirmations is relevant across all spheres of life. If your goal is to run three miles in the morning, the affirmation could be, "As my health is important to me and my family, I run three miles every morning." It is about stating your affirmations in the present tense, as if you are already doing and achieving that goal. The reason they need to be as such is because the subconscious mind cannot differentiate between past and future. It does not know the difference between *yes* or *no* either. It simply reacts as if it is truth. That is why affirmations are stated positively and as though each statement is true right now.

To write your affirmations, follow these guidelines:

- Personal. Affirmations are written with the word *I* in them. You can only affirm for yourself.
- Positive. Always describe what you want in your affirmation. Describe what you want to move forward toward, not what you want to move away from.
- Present Tense. Affirmations are written as though they are happening right now.
- Indicate Achievement. Eliminate words such as *can, will, should,* and *want.* Include phrases like "I am," "I do," or "I have."
- No Comparison. Comparing yourself to others is ineffective. This is a personal process and based on you.
- Action Words. Use terms that trigger action, such as *easily, quickly, thrive on, energetically,* or *confidently.*
- Emotion Words. The more positive emotion you feel when you are picturing an accomplished goal, the faster the affirmation will work for you.
- Accuracy. Be specific. If your affirmation is to exercise, describe what type and when you exercise.
- Balance. Establish affirmations that balance all aspects of your life.
- Visualize. After you have set your affirmations, close your eyes and visualize them. See yourself achieving them. The

clearer you can visualize the desired state, the greater the possibility of positive change.

- Confidential. Only share them with those who will support you.

If some of your goals are to lose 15 pounds in three months, hold family dinners a minimum of four nights a week, or have date nights with your spouse/partner twice a month, here are some potential affirmations:

- As I am a corporate athlete and am focused on my health and well-being, I walk for exercise five days a week and weigh my target weight of xxx pounds.
- As the children are growing up way too fast, we have dinner as a family a minimum of four nights a week.
- As I love him/her more than ever, we celebrate our lives together with a date night twice a month.

Whatever your affirmations are, they will need to become part of your daily routine. Personally, I repeat my affirmations first thing every morning and last thing every night. Now, please trust me, this is not to say I never deviate from my stated affirmations, but it is to say when I do deviate, my subconscious mind is knocking on the door and saying, "That is not you."

Another key element of the affirmation process is visualization. There are two forms of visualization—intentional, as part of saying your affirmations, and passive, in terms of merely having them out in front of you. Regarding intentional visualization, as you state your affirmations, clearly see yourself in the future state. As outlined above, if one of your affirmations is "As the children are growing up way too fast, we have dinner as a family a minimum of four nights a week," see yourself sitting around the table with your family while you state this. The more vivid your visualization, the more powerful the tool becomes to create change.

You can also use passive stimulation. Our memories are much stronger when we see things in real life as opposed to hearing them.

The more you see, the faster you will internalize. Whether it is your vision, values, or affirmations, put them out in your line of sight, where you can see them often. Bedroom, study, bathroom mirror, or your computer—find a place that keeps them visible. What is interesting about the brain is that even if you do not look at something intently every day, you will still benefit from that visualization. A team of researchers from the UK—Anthony Blanchfield, James Hardy, and Sameule Marcora[47]—studied the impact of these unconscious visual cues on the perception of their cycling effort. They conducted two experiments. In experiment one, thirteen individuals were subliminally primed with happy or sad faces as they cycled to exhaustion. Results showed that individuals cycled for a significantly longer duration when unconsciously primed with happy faces. Similarly, in experiment two, subliminal priming with "action words" facilitated a significantly longer time before exhaustion.

As a personal example, when the children were living at home, I printed out our family vision and values on one page and hung it in all the bedrooms in the house. It served as a constant reminder of who we wanted to be as a family. At times you will wonder if your children are even paying attention to it. In my case, I noticed one of the first positive signs when one of our daughters had to do show-and-tell at school. She came home, ran to her bedroom, took the framed vision and values off the wall, and put it in her backpack. More than ten years later, when in high school she had to write a paper on leadership covering something that had positively affected her in life, she turned to the very same framed document.

Keep in mind, visualization is not about wishing and hoping something will happen as a fantasy, but rather it is future-oriented and grounded in reality

Athletes use this to do everything from simulating practice to overcoming fear and even recovering from an injury. Have you ever watched major championship winner Jason Day close his eyes before he steps up to the golf ball? He is visualizing his shot. By visualizing as you state your affirmations and looking at the reminders constantly, you stir the emotions and increase the likelihood of achieving your goal.

Daily Prescription

To create a new habit, there is general agreement that you have to repeat the behavior for 30–45 days. It is like following a daily prescription. Just as your doctor gives you a prescription with exact specifics, the same is true for non-medication-related situations. Ed Foreman, in his Successful Life course, talks about the importance of this. His theory is that if you follow a focused prescription for seven days, you will have a great week; then for four weeks and you will have a great month; then for 12 months and you will have a great year; and then for the rest of your life.

Key elements of my daily prescription while still working at Caterpillar were the following:

- Affirmations and prayers first thing in the morning
- Followed by exercise routine
- Then a healthful breakfast and cleaning of emails
- In the office by 7:15 a.m.
- Healthful snack at 10:00 a.m. and 2:00 p.m.
- Salad with protein for lunch
- Dinner with the family
- Cleaning of emails after dinner
- Before bed, repetition of affirmations

Now, my schedule did not allow me to do this every day, but it was always in the back of my mind. The greatest derailers for me were transitions that involved a change in location and job. As I fought to get back on track, it was the affirmations that led the way in getting me back there. Lay out your daily prescription and understand that the more consistently you execute it, the more it will lead to the habits you are after. Take a look at Appendix 2, page 124, which captures the daily prescription from Ed Foreman's Successful Life course. As you attempt to develop your own, it can serve as a good thought provoker. As Ed used to say, "Which side of the menu do you want to choose today?"

Accountability

The last step in the process is to keep track regularly. As emphasized throughout, it is all about creating visibility and awareness to keep things at the conscious level. Monitor your progress. See for yourself if your actions are inching you toward your goals or not. Adjust your tactics if not. Try different approaches until you find yourself getting closer and closer to your goals. That is why constant evaluation daily is critical. If you do not track, you cannot measure your progress.

For me this was as simple as keeping a calendar in my workout room where I marked the days I exercised and gave my diet a grade. That month, I could look up and visibly see if I was following my affirmations and plans relative to diet and exercise. This was supported by weighing in every Monday and Friday morning. You can hold yourself accountable through a calendar, an app, or other ways to measure actual versus planned results, but you have to keep score. In the words of Stephen Covey, "Accountability breeds response-ability."

Tying It All Together

The only way to tie the concepts of discipline leading to habits together is to take them for a test drive. Think through where you are regarding how you live and lead. Assess the balance you have in your life. Critique where you stand on having authentic relationships at all levels of the organization. Determine if you have an operating model that yields desired results. Then, based on this review, pick out one or two changes you want to make and run them through the process—goal/actions, affirmations, daily prescription, accountability. Your understanding and appreciation of the process will not come from the written words; it will come from seeing positive change. If you stick with it, over time it will become an integral part of how you live and lead.

I do a complete review of my goals, actions, and affirmations annually between Christmas and New Year—a yearly quality check on who I was during the year compared with who I wanted to be and the establishment of updates to my goals, actions, affirmations, and daily prescription to keep me on the right path. As I reflect, this process has shaped not only who I have been as a leader but also as a person, husband and father. I went back into my personal files and found my affirmations from more than 20 years ago (2000):

> We will positively impact the people and responsibilities experienced throughout life.
>
> As I love her more each day, I have a positive and romantic relationship with my wife, Ann, as we raise three positive, contributing children and successfully launch them into adulthood.
>
> As I am an active listener, in interacting with Ann, the children, and others, I listen and use positive and constructive language and comments.
>
> I am a vice president at Caterpillar known for my leadership, development, and communication skills as well as my ability to balance requirements between home and work and build great leaders around me.
>
> As I love what I do, I never complain about the hours, work, or travel, and I look forward to going to work each day. I maintain a positive, levelheaded attitude and support those around me. I wear a smile on my face; life is good.
>
> Because I will live to 100 and spoil my grandchildren, I watch what I eat and watch what I drink as I feed this vibrant, dynamic body. I drink 60 ounces of water a day and no more than one cup of coffee and one glass of wine. I eat healthful foods. Exceptions are allowed no more than once a week.
>
> Because I am a corporate athlete, I enjoy getting up early. I exercise daily and weigh my

target weight of 170 with a 34-inch waist and the proper cholesterol balance. I continue to improve my flexibility, stamina, and strength.

Because I have so much to be thankful for and want to give thanks to the Lord, I go to church weekly. The Lord has created this day; let us rejoice and give praise. He will look out over my family, and He will look out over me. I ask this through your name, oh Lord, Jesus Christ, as through you all things are possible.

Now, the ultimate judges of how I have done in living up to the above affirmations from 20 years ago are those around me. But as I do my own assessment, it does bolster my confidence in the process, leading to my belief that it can make a difference for you. Once again, a caution: start small with a focus on a few areas you want to change and develop new habits. From this you gain confidence and expand your areas of focus. Create a draft set of plans in Appendix 1, page 123, as a starting point.

Hitting the Curve

Smooth seas do not make skillful sailors.

—African proverb

First pitch, Wrigley Field, August 11, 2016

As I had been a lifelong St. Louis Cardinals fan, it was a unique opportunity to throw out the first pitch at the home of their archrivals, the Chicago Cubs. The opportunity was a gift from a great friend and Caterpillar board member. When he presented me with the gift, I asked him, "Is it okay if I wear a St. Louis Cardinals jersey?" to which he replied, "I'm not sure that will work." With the challenge at hand, the last thing I was worried about was the local Chicago Cubs' fans giving a Cardinals' fan a hard time, but I did compromise and wore a Cat® shirt. While I did throw out the first pitch, since then I have moved on to trying to hit the curve.

It is one thing to be a good leader when times are good, but quite another during a crisis. In reality, we all have gone or will be going through our own share of challenges. How does one deal with the curveballs life throws at us?

The focus of this final chapter is on two points:

1. In life, everyone faces adversity in some size, shape, or form. The time to start preparing for a curveball in life is not when it is leaving the pitcher's hand but way before. It begins with how we live and lead each and every day, starting today.
2. In the end, none of us will be measured by the adversity in our lives. We will all be measured by how we responded to that situation.

One of my many great joys in life is the sensation of a good morning run. I started jogging after my freshman year in college, after I had gained ten pounds eating dormitory food, and never stopped. Later, there was nothing I enjoyed more than jogging with our son, Jay. We started jogging together when he was about five years old. He would ride his bike, and I had to push him up the hills. Over time, it evolved to our running side by side and then, eventually, to the point where I was the one who had trouble keeping up. Today, we have gone full circle: He jogs and I now ride my three-wheel bike.

It was on one of these morning runs in December 2014 when I had the first indication that something was not quite right. It was between Christmas and New Year's, and our family had gathered for the holidays in North Carolina, where two of our three children lived. Jay and I were out on a morning run, and shortly after we started, my left toe would catch about every fifteen steps. In the beginning I thought it was probably just a pinched nerve, as I had just come off a long flight from Singapore. But as we continued to jog over the holidays, the problem did not go away. Ann and our children pushed me to get to the bottom of the issue. This started a ten-month journey of multiple doctors, physical therapists, acupuncture, chiropractors, x-rays, MRIs, and many more tests. However, none of them were able to identify the root cause.

In early September 2015, one of the doctors turned to me and said, "The one thing we have not checked is neurology." He suggested that I go to the Mayo Clinic in Rochester, Minnesota, and the appointment was set for early November. I clearly understood that I had an issue, as it had become extremely difficult to jog. I had stiffness in my left leg and had developed weakness in my left ankle. I was committed to discovering the root cause and then getting on a path to full recovery.

While we had our share of challenges on life's journey, we never expected the realities of November 5, 2015. After three days of testing, the head neurologist pulled us into his office. He asked if I knew what he was going to do, and I responded, "You are going to help figure out what is going on." His response was, "No, I'm the one who is going to tell you that you have Amyotrophic Lateral Sclerosis." ALS is more commonly known as Lou Gehrig's disease after it killed the 37-year-old Hall of Fame baseball legend in 1941. It was a stunning moment for me and my wife, Ann. And, one that we will never forget.

While I had been aware of the disease, one of the first thoughts that ran through my mind was, how could this even be possible? Two sick days in my 37 years at Caterpillar, in good health, focused on diet as well as exercise—this could not be happening. As I relayed this message to the doctor, his response was, "That's a fairly normal profile for an ALS patient."

There are many things from that conversation that still stay with me today. I asked the doctor, "How do we fight this thing— diet, exercise, and more?" His response was, "It doesn't work that way. You are going to come back every three months and we will monitor your strength and breathing capacity, and after getting three or four readings, we'll be able to roughly project how long you have to live. In all likelihood, it will be in the two- to five-year range."

My wife, out of frustration, asked the doctor, "What should we do?" The doctor said, "Make a list of all places in the world you would like to go and go now." To which I responded, "I've already been there." Going places was not high on my list; making the most out of whatever time I had left was.

This was a massive life event for us. The hardest part was telling our children and parents. We had always operated as a close-knit family, so we waited until Thanksgiving with all the children together to make some major decisions. These included the following:

1. What should I do about Caterpillar? I was one of the candidates to be the next CEO. However, I quickly concluded that I could either help run Caterpillar or fight the disease. I could not do both. I also stayed true to what I had always believed. It is never about the individual; it is always about the enterprise, and the right thing to do for the enterprise was for me to step down and let the next capable leader step up.

2. Were we going to be open about the disease or only say I was retiring? This was a fairly easy decision. In leading employees or engaging customers, dealers, or suppliers, I think I was known for being open and transparent. I always believed transparency builds trust, and therefore, I chose to be open and transparent about my ALS diagnosis.

3. Lastly, were we going to simply fight the disease or get involved in the broader ALS fight? Once again, this was a fairly easy decision. My time at Caterpillar had taught me a lot and opened up a network that I could leverage to help make a difference. It also tied back to our family vision: "To positively impact the people and responsibilities experienced throughout life." If I was going to set the right example for our family, I had to engage in the broader fight.

After processing the initial shock of the diagnosis, I quickly reverted to the practices outlined in this book to take on the new challenge at hand. This leads to the second point of this chapter, that none of us will be measured by the adversities in our lives but rather by how we respond to them. I have no interest in being remembered for having ALS, but I have a strong interest in making a difference in what is a tough disease.

In the past six-plus years, it has become even more clear that my only defense versus the negative side of the diagnosis is a strong offense. My mind sometimes wanders to where I would be if I had not planned my life with intention and rigor.

- Where would I be without my faith and strong relationships with family and friends?
- Where would I be if I had come into the disease weak or out of shape?
- Where would I be if I did not understand the importance of discipline and creating new habits?

Personally and as a family, we are using the tools outlined in this book to take on the challenge at hand. Professionally, I chair the advisory board of Answer ALS, the largest and most comprehensive ALS research project in history. My involvement in the project started as a patient but later broadened to participation in funding the project through Stay Strong (staystrongvsals.com). Then, through my engagement with the doctors leading the project, it expanded to chair of the advisory board back in 2017.

As I reflect, it is the balance that I had in my life coming into the disease that has had the greatest impact. Because of that balance, I have the clarity of thought and stability to navigate the challenge at hand and plan my future. My vision statement remains the same—to positively impact the people and responsibilities experienced throughout life. I continue to be disciplined in focusing on my health, managing my calendar, balancing my time between trying to make a difference in ALS, building a property development business with our son, and spending quality time with family and friends. Efficiency continues to set me free, and I have transitioned from being a corporate athlete to an ALS athlete.

On relationships, when you have a position within a company that affords you a degree of authority, you always wonder if the relationships you have built will stand the test of time well beyond your career. The last six plus years have demonstrated to me that if those relationships are built on a foundation of mutual trust and respect, they stand the test of time. I remain amazed at the strength of our support network, all the way from family and friends to work colleagues to dealers, suppliers, and customers. Their support helped me navigate the transition to the next phase as I try to make a difference in the world of ALS research. Following the announcement of my retirement and our plan to engage in the broader ALS fight, dealers and suppliers from around the world donated more than $4 million to Stay Strong, a dollar figure matched by Caterpillar. This, combined with commitments from our family and friends, has led to an impact of more than $14 million supporting research and bringing better assistive technologies to those suffering from the disease, as of the end of 2021.

My diagnosis has also opened up new relationships. My uncle Art used to say, "There is no ill wind that blows so hard that it doesn't blow some good." One of the gifts of my diagnosis is the new people I have met that I never would have otherwise. Using many of the practices outlined earlier in the book, I have had the blessing of building some wonderful relationships. Through Answer ALS, I have engaged with people at all levels of the project, ranging from some of the world's leading neurologists to the amazing nurses that care for people in the ALS clinics and enroll patients into the program. I get my hands dirty doing some of the heavy lifting, especially in the area of fundraising. I have totally "unpacked my bags," as this has become a life calling. I continue to advocate for the "simultaneous lift" with incredible support from the likes of Microsoft and IBM. And lastly, I bring the same predictability to leading Answer ALS as I did at Caterpillar. Many of these principles are now quoted in the halls of Johns Hopkins, Northwestern, and Cedars-Sinai. As I said earlier, while there are challenges that come with the disease, there are also gifts. And a big part of those are the relationships I have built on this journey.

The operating model is also very relevant in the world of ALS. As of the writing of this book, the team has completed patient and control enrollment, built the portal, started the process of releasing the rich data to the world of ALS researchers, and raised $45 million to fund the project. In the simplest of terms, we are building the haystack and then enabling the global research community and analytics, artificial intelligence, machine learning, and new emerging technologies to discover the needle—the subgroups and pathways that cause this disease. I remain convinced that until we understand the root cause, any drug trial is a shot in the dark. While it is different from building tractors, the principles of an operating model easily transfer to the world of neuroscience.

Lastly, I continue to use the techniques outlined to create positive change leading to new habits. I was diagnosed on November 5, 2015, and I rewrote my goals and affirmations on November 7 to include the following:

- Outlive my parents and in-laws—there is nothing more painful than a parent burying a child.
- Walk our daughters down the aisle—neither daughter was married when I was diagnosed.
- Actively engage with our grandsons—I wanted them to know their Papa.
- Make a difference in what is a tough disease—Caterpillar was a good teacher, and I wanted to apply the lessons learned to the world of ALS.
- Refuse to be defined by my diagnosis—there is more to life than fighting the disease.

From the goals came action plans, such as adjustments to my exercise routine, an even more disciplined diet, a focus on actively engaging in the world of ALS, and more. This process led me to new affirmations that continue to evolve:

I positively impact the people and responsibilities experienced throughout life.

I continue to heal through a strong faith and disciplined thought, diet, and exercise.

I beat the odds versus ALS. I am the exception, and I outlive my parents and in-laws, grow old with Ann, walk my daughters down the aisle and dance the father-daughter dance. I teach my grandchildren to play golf and walk the course the first time Cole beats Jay. Leo and I continue to build on the story we will tell one day.

I play a leadership role in the world of ALS. There is no disease that has evolved for which our Creator will not help in finding a cure. I increase awareness and attract investment, supporting those in search of a cure and those bringing better, more assistive technology to people suffering from the disease.

I am strong and healthy and build my daily routine around a healthful lifestyle. I fully adhere to the Wahls Protocol, as food is my fuel, and eliminate gluten, dairy, and processed sugar from my diet. I execute my daily exercise routine focused on my gait, balance, strength, and flexibility. As rest is important for my health, I get my required sleep.

I maintain a single-digit golf handicap index, execute the simplification plan, expand our development business, and pass on lessons learned to the next generation of leaders.

Through it all, I maintain my strong faith and never forget the Lord has created this day; let us rejoice and give praise. He will look out over my family, and He will look out over me. I ask this through your name, Lord Jesus Christ, as through you all things are possible.

Together, these steps have led to a new, disciplined protocol or, as described earlier, daily prescription for me. I start every day with prayers and affirmations, and then I head downstairs to my exercise room and do a routine called foundation training, focused on the major muscle groups that this disease affects. I add cardio in the afternoons through swimming or the elliptical.

My diet is gluten-free, dairy-free, and processed-sugar-free. I measure toxicity in my body regularly and cleanse as required because our bodies are not designed for the environmental factors we introduce into everyday life.

I finish the day once again with my prayers and affirmations and then get my targeted eight hours of sleep.

Now, do not for a minute think that at all times I feel I have things under control. Following my ALS diagnosis, I do sometimes get down and wonder what would have happened if I had finished out my career at Caterpillar. I get frustrated when one of the grandsons says, "Let's play tag," and it is just impossible for me to do so. However, when I am tempted to go to a dark place, I turn to the practices and principles outlined in this book. When facing the curveballs of life, I remain convinced the only defense is a good offense.

To date, I am staying strong. While originally given two to five years to live, I am approaching the seven-year mark. I am still on my feet with the help of two walking crutches, and my strength and breathing capacity have been steady. As my neurologist says, I am an outlier. I often get the question, "Why?" This is my response:

- First, I do think I have a slower-advancing form of the disease. Being close to a lot of ALS patients, it reinforces the hypothesis we are trying to prove out that there is not one form of this disease.
- Secondly, I do believe the discipline and execution of a protocol focused on diet, exercise, and a naturopathic approach to health have had a huge impact.
- Lastly, I believe that the good Lord senses I am trying to make a difference and He wants me to finish what I have started. It is not that I am afraid of where I am going; it is more that I so love where I am. Perhaps in a strange way, the last six plus years have been some of the best years of my life.

My purpose in sharing how the concepts outlined in this book also apply to adversity is to help prepare you for the eventual curveball life may throw at you, be it work or home-related. Whether it is loss of a loved one, loss of a job, a missed promotion, or even navigating through a pandemic, the same principles stand the test of time.

In no way do I think I have this all figured out, but as I have dealt with my own adversity and observed others who have dealt with it firsthand, here are some of the common themes:

- Live and lead with focus and a purpose, as I have attempted to outline in this book. I always believed it before ALS, and I believe it even more today. Do not wait until adversity comes knocking on your door.

- Have a strong faith. As I have observed, a strong faith has given close friends who lost loved ones the strength to prevail. Everybody processes faith in his or her own way. Some say I was given ALS by God so I could help make a difference. I see it differently. The good Lord does not give someone a disease or take a young person from this earth before their time, but He does give us the strength to take on the challenges of life.

- Refuse to accept a victim's mentality—do not fall into the trap of convincing yourself you are a victim, because if you do, it is a slippery slope of despair. Adversity is easy to see; opportunity is a much harder find. It took me years to focus on things I could control versus those out of my control. The reality is, I have ALS, and unfortunately, there is nothing I can do about it. My attention only adds value when it is focused on things I can control. This is where affirmations and discipline play a key role.

- Be your own advocate, especially if the adversity is on the health front. Get a second opinion. Do not accept the "There is nothing you can do about it" advice. I subscribe to the foundation of Chinese medicine: The body is designed to heal itself when given the right conditions. Yes, I marvel at the miracles of modern medicine, but I also embrace concepts from nontraditional approaches.

- How you respond directly affects others. I remember attending the funeral of a dear ALS colleague, Jay Fishman. What struck me from the service was the impact Jay's response to the disease had on those around him. He told me early on, "You have a choice: you can stay in bed, or you can stay engaged." And engaged he was. The way he handled the disease eased the burden for everyone around him and made the service a celebration of his life.

- Understand that you are not in it alone. In a recent presentation I gave on dealing with adversity, in the Q&A someone asked me what I feared the most. I told him that my greatest fear was the loss of independence, of having to depend on others to take care of me, as I had spent a good portion of my life attempting to take care of others. But like me, you will have to learn to accept the fact that you have others who want to support and take care of you.

Finally, a Buddhist quote that has really begun to resonate is, "Every end is a new beginning." This has started to come to light as I have gone on my ALS journey. Other than my father, probably the person most disappointed by the circumstances that led to my retirement was my father-in-law, Dale Athey. Yes, he was my father-in-law but also a dear friend. Shortly before he passed away, he came to Raleigh for our daughter Stefanie's wedding. After the wedding, he stayed a couple of weeks, and in one of our conversations, he told me how he and his fellow parishioners at United Methodist Church in Peoria felt my story, my diagnosis, was such a sad one. I told him that I did not agree. I truly do think I made a difference at Caterpillar, and now I have the opportunity to make a difference in what is a tough disease. And if I make a difference at Caterpillar and with Answer ALS in my one lifetime, I will consider it a great life fulfilling the vision "to positively impact the people and responsibilities experienced throughout life."

Remember that none of us are going to get out of this alive. We won't be measured by events, announcements, job titles, personal challenges, or even a diagnosis. We will be measured by how we respond and the contributions we make. And in all this, I simply want a passing grade.

I really do want to thank you for joining in the discussion. As I always say in closing, "You stay strong, and I'll do the same."

Key Takeaways

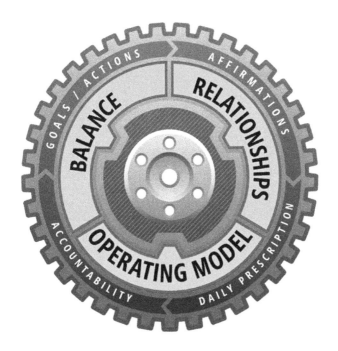

I will finish the book as I opened it, by reemphasizing four key points.

On balance, pursuit of a professional career at the expense of everything and everyone else can lead to a shallow victory. I acknowledge that life is rarely in perfect balance, but you have to be consciously aware of your state and work toward bringing it into balance. Fighting for this balance requires a plan, introducing efficiencies and becoming a "corporate athlete"—taking care of your physical, emotional, and mental well-being.

Your ability to lead and inspire is dependent on building relationships across the organization and by demonstrating you really do care about your people. This is all the more important because the higher you move up the organization, the greater the number of filters between you and the truth. To overcome these barriers and deliver results, build relationships by showing you care, unpacking your bags, getting your hands dirty, and integrating this activity into your calendar.

To remain relevant, you need an operating model that constantly evaluates the external environment, selects priorities, and drives execution. To drive value as a leader, you need a disciplined approach to providing your entire team with an unequivocal clarity of direction focused on the few things that will make the biggest difference.

As you deploy the components of the flywheel, it will require a heightened level of discipline leading to habits. Theories state that it takes something in the range of 30–45 days to develop new habits. If you want to change a behavior, it all starts with developing new habits.

I hope the flywheel framework will encourage you to develop a model that works for you. As I stated upfront, there are several ways to get to a destination. The flywheel is not an explicit prescription but a framework you can use to mold your own approach. I encourage you to use these ideas as a starting point to create your own path. As you proceed, do not attempt to deploy all the concepts at once, but take them slowly, one at a time. Take them for a test drive; there is no better time to begin than now.

To help you get started, complete an assessment of where you stand today. Do you have good balance in your life? Do you have meaningful relationships at all levels of the organization? Do you have a model that enables the people in your organization to clearly understand the role they play? Determine your initial areas of focus from your assessment, and then apply the suggested techniques to drive discipline and develop new habits. Just like the flywheel, it all starts by putting things in motion, and you will see results and build confidence, momentum, and sustainable habits.

The journey is not an easy one, but the benefits far outweigh the effort. Step back and think about where you want to be professionally and personally in ten or 20 years. I remain convinced getting your own flywheel started now is important to achieving your goals and enjoying the advantages of living and leading based on an explicit plan. The last thing any of us wants is to reflect on life with regret.

Appendix 1

Self-Assessment

On a scale of 1–5, where 5 means Agree and 1 means Disagree, please rate the following:

- ✓ I am satisfied with the balance in my life. ___
- ✓ I have a defined personal vision. ___
- ✓ I focus on my physical and mental health. ___
- ✓ I have explicit goals and action items to lead my life. ___
- ✓ I hold myself accountable by tracking my results versus the plan. ___
- ✓ I have built strong relationships across all levels of the organization. ___
- ✓ I build relationships and engage with the entire organizational value chain. ___
- ✓ I work through a well-defined framework or operating model. ___
- ✓ I have a granular understanding of my business. ___
- ✓ I effectively cascade priorities and set cadence at work. ___

If you rate more 1s, 2s, or 3s, pick the area where you want to start and focus on improving it first.

Self-Improvement Goals—list the focus areas, goals, and actions you will you take.

Focus Areas	Goals	Actions
1.	▪ ▪	▪ ▪ ▪ ▪
2.	▪ ▪	▪ ▪ ▪ ▪
3.	▪ ▪	▪ ▪ ▪ ▪

Appendix 2

LIFE'S DAILY MENU*
WHICH DO YOU CHOOSE TODAY?

MENU
HOW TO HAVE A "TERRIFIC" DAY

APPETIZER	**FARE**
Awaken Early	Appreciation for Life
Inspirational Reading	Good News Immediately
Early Morning Walk or Run	Smiles & Enthusiasm
Devotion & Thanksgiving	Recognition & Expectation
Brief Regular Exercise	Vibrant Health & Strong Body
Positive Podcast	Vision & Encouragement
Shower & Readiness	Freshness & Anticipation

ENTREE
Nourishing Breakfast (25%) | Alertness, Energy, Vitality
Multi-Vitamin + E + C + A | Energy, Vitality, Immunity
Wholesome, Positive Thoughts | Accomplishment & Wealth
Pleasant Greetings to Everyone | Many Friends & Happiness
Give Sincere Appreciation | Love, Honor & Cooperation
Listen More, Talk Less | Respect, Approval, Knowledge
Plan for the Day & Future | Creativity & Organization
Do One Task at a Time | Accomplish Greatly
See Your Work as Pleasurable | Outstanding Achievement
Moderate Lunch (50%) | Alive, Alert & Awake
Work/Rest/Work/Rest | Prosperity & Satisfaction

(Mind-Controlled Relaxation)
Count Your Blessings | Abundance, Love & Serenity
Play & Relaxation | Happiness & Enjoyment
Moderation & Temperance | Clear, Calm & Organized
Reasonable Dinner (25%) | Comfortable & Relaxed

DESSERT
Review Your Accomplishments | Peace of Mind & Success
Prayer | Homage & Self-Confidence
Relax & Sleep | Sweet Dreams & Full Life

*Taken from Ed Foreman's Successful Life Course

MENU
HOW TO HAVE A "BAD" DAY

APPETIZER   **FARE**

Awaken Late (Have to Rush) .... Anxiety & Bitterness
Go Get Newspaper (Like a Dog) .... Mostly Bad News
Digest Bad News on the Run .... Feel Bad & Get Mad
No Devotion or Inspiration.................................... Low Spirit, Easily Offended
No Exercise .... Sluggish, Tired & Run Down
Radio or Television Report .... Disaster, Trouble & Despair
Too Late to Get Bath... Sleepy, Stinky & Unkempt

ENTREE

No Breakfast or Coffee & Donut .... Hungry, Mean & Nervous
Cigarette, Candy, Cola .... Hacking Cough & Indigestion
Negative, Derogatory Thought.............................. Problems & Depression
Unfriendly & Ugly to Others .... Few or No Friends
Criticize, Condemn & Complain .... Condemnation, No Love
Dictate, Direct & Demand.................................... Disrespect & Ridicule
No Plans for the Day or Future .... Disorganized & Sour
Tackle Everything at Once .... Confusion & Disorder
See Your Job as Necessary Evil .... Barely Get By
Lunch-Greasy & Hurried .... Drowsy, Gassy & Dull
Work/Work/Work/Work.. Little Money & Fatigue
(Stay Too Busy to Rest & Relax)
Curse Life & Gripe .... Poverty, Hate & Worry
No Play & No Relaxation .... Tension & Frustration
Indulgence & Dissipation .... Illness, Tired, No Confidence
Dinner-Drink & Eat Heavy .... Burp, Barf & Nightmares

DESSERT

Worry, Fret & Be Tense.. Sickness, Fear & Failure
No Prayer of Thanksgiving.................................... Selfish, Resentful & Jealous
Stay Uptight & Poor Sleep .... Bad Dreams & Half-Life

References

1   Viktor Frankl, *Man's Search for Meaning* (Boston: Beacon Press, 1946).
2   https://www.bls.gov/tus/charts/.
3   https://www.cnbc.com/2017/05/03/how-the-8-hour-workday-changed-how-americans-work.html.
4   https://healthcareers.co/work-life-balance-statistics/.
5   S. Peck, *The Road Less Travelled* (1978).
6   S. Covey, The 7 Habits of Highly Effective People (Free Press, 1989).
7   W. T. Gallwey, *The Inner Game of Work: Focus, Learning, Pleasure, and Mobility in the Workplace* (Random House, 2001).
8   A. Jain, Burnout: Beat Fatigue to Thrive in an Overworked World (Penguin Random House, 2019).
9   https://www.bls.gov/news.release/pdf/famee.pdf.
10 M. E. Eisenberg, R. E. Olson, D. Neumark-Sztainer, M. Story, and L. H. Bearinger, "Correlations between Family Meals and Psychosocial Well-Being Among Adolescents," *Archives of Pediatrics & Adolescent Medicine* 158 (8), 792–796.
11 B. Feiler, *The Secrets of Happy Families: Improve Your Mornings, Tell Your Family History, Fight Smarter, Go Out and Play, and Much More* (William Morrow Paperbacks, 2013).
12 M. Zawadzki, J. Smyth, and H. Costigan, "Real-Time Associations Between Engaging in Leisure and Daily Health and Well-Being," *Annals of Behavioral Medicine: A Publication of the Society of Behavioral Medicine* 49 (4), 605–615.
13 S. D. Pressman and S. Cohen, "Does Positive Affect Influence Health?" *Psychological Bulletin* 131, 925–71.
14 G. E. Vaillant, "Aging Well: Surprising Guideposts to a Happier Life," *Landmark Study of Adult Development* (2008).
15 R. M. Kaplan and R. G. Kronick, "Marital Status and Longevity in the United States Population," *Journal of Epidemiology & Community Health*, 760–65.
16 D. Stevens, G. Kiger, and P. J. Riley, "Working Hard and Hardly Working: Domestic Labor and Marital Satisfaction Among Dual-Earner Couples," *Journal of Marriage and Family* 63 (2), 514–526.
17 https://hbr.org/2017/04/employee-burnout-is-a-problem-with-the-company-not-the-person.
18 D. Jorgenson, M. Ho, and K. Stiroh, "A Retrospective Look at the US Productivity Growth Resurgence," *Journal of Economic Perspectives* 22 (1), 3–24.

[19] G. Mark, D. Gudith, and U. Klocke, "The Cost of Interrupted Work: More Speed and Stress," proceedings of the SIGCHI conference on Human Factors in Computing Systems (April 2008), 107–110.

[20] https://blog.dscout.com/mobile-touches.

[21] https://www.irishtimes.com/life-and-style/health-family/parenting/how-technology-and-social-media-is-undermining-family-relationships-1.3568291#ssm.

[22] A. F. Ward, K. Duke, A. Gneezy, and M. W. Bos, "Brain Drain: The Mere Presence of One's Own Smartphone Reduces Available Cognitive Capacity," *Journal of the Association for Consumer Research* 2.2, 140–54.

[23] L. A. Perlow and J. L. Porter, "Making Time Off Predictable—and Required," *Harvard Business Review* 87.10, 102–09.

[24] E. Gonzalez-Mulé, http://archive.inside.indiana.edu/editors-picks/research/2016-10-19-stressful-work-environment.shtml.

[25] https://www.orlandohealth.com/content-hub/americans-are-gaining-weight-every-decade.

[26] K. M. Kniffin, B. Wansink, C. M. Devine, and J. Sobal, "Eating Together at the Firehouse: How Workplace Commensality Relates to the Performance of Firefighters," *Human Performance* 28.4, 281–306.

[27] J. A. Fulkerson, J. Strauss, D. Neumark-Sztainer, M. Story, and K. Boutelle, "Correlates of Psychosocial Well-Being among Overweight Adolescents: The Role of the Family," *Journal of Consulting and Clinical Psychology* 75 (1), 181.

[28] F. J. Penedo and J. R. Dahn, "Exercise and Well-Being: A Review of Mental and Physical Health Benefits Associated with Physical Activity," *Current Opinion in Psychiatry* 18.2, 189–93.

[29] C. Crowley and H. S. Lodge, *Younger Next Year: Live Strong, Fit, and Sexy—Until You're 80 and Beyond* (Workman Publishing, 2007).

[30] C. L. Hogan, J. Mata, and L. L. Carstensen, "Exercise Holds Immediate Benefits for Affect and Cognition in Younger and Older Adults," *Psychology and Aging* 28 (2), 587.

[31] L. T. Hoyt, M. G. Craske, S. Mineka, and E. K. Adam, "Positive and Negative Affect and Arousal: Cross-Sectional and Longitudinal Associations with Adolescent Cortisol Diurnal Rhythms," *Psychosomatic Medicine*, 77 (4), 392.

[32] https://www.sleepfoundation.org/press-release/national-sleep-foundation-brings-awareness-dangers-falling-asleep-wheel.

[33] https://www.zdnet.com/article/americans-consume-100000-words-of-information-each-day-study-says/.

[34] https://qz.com/150577/an-average-nfl-game-more-than-100-commercials-and-just-11-minutes-of-play/.

[35] R. A. Emmons and M. E. McCullough, "Counting Blessings versus Burdens: An Experimental Investigation of Gratitude and Subjective Well-Being in Daily Life," *Journal of Personality and Social Psychology*, 84 (2).

[36] E. Foreman, *The Power of Living by Design* (2013).

REFERENCES

37 R. L. Cross, R. L. Cross, and A. Parker, *The Hidden Power of Social Networks: Understanding How Work Really Gets Done in Organizations* (Harvard Business Press, 2004).

38 K. Cameron, *Positive Leadership: Strategies for Extraordinary Performance* (Berrett-Koehler Publishers, 2012).

39 M. Worline and J. E. Dutton, *Awakening Compassion at Work: The Quiet Power That Elevates People and Organizations* (Berrett-Koehler Publishers, 2017).

40 J. Collins, *Good to Great: Why Some Companies Make the Leap and Others Don't* (Harper Collins, 2001).

41 S. Gillis, L. Mergy, and J. Shalleck, *Beliefs, Behaviors, and Results: The Chief Executive's Guide to Delivering Superior Shareholder Value* (Greenleaf Book Group Press, 2013).

42 W. Taylor, Simply Brilliant: How Great Organizations Do Ordinary Things in Extraordinary Ways (Portfolio, 2016).

43 https://www.wbay.com/content/news/Research-shows-up-to-80-percent-of-New-Years-resolutions-fail-by-mid-February-567530441.html.

44 S. Gardner and D. Albee (2015). Study focuses on strategies for achieving goals, resolutions.

45 P. R. Harris, K. Mayle, L. Mabbott, and L. Napper, "Self-Affirmation Reduces Smokers' Defensiveness to Graphic On-Pack Cigarette Warning Labels," *Health Psychology* 26, 437–46.

46 C. J. Armitage, P. R. Harris, G. Hepton, and L. Napper, "Self-Affirmation Increases Acceptance of Health-Risk Information Among UK Adult Smokers with Low Socioeconomic Status," *Psychology of Addictive Behaviors* 22, 88–95.

47 A. Blanchfield, J. Hardy, and S. Marcora, "Non-Conscious Visual Cues Related to Affect and Action Alter Perception of Effort and Endurance Performance," *Frontiers in Human Neuroscience* 8, 967.

About the Authors

Ed Rapp retired from Caterpillar Inc. in July 2016. Prior to his retirement, Ed was a Caterpillar Inc. group president. During his time in the Caterpillar Executive Office, he led Resource Industries and Construction Industries and was the company's CFO.

Rapp has more than 37 years of global experience and has lived and worked in the United States, Africa, Europe, and Asia. Rapp's expertise extends to finance, marketing, dealer development, manufacturing, and product development.

Rapp's career was cut short when he was diagnosed with Amyotrophic Lateral Sclerosis, or ALS, also known as Lou Gehrig's disease, in late 2015. Ed founded Stay Strong vs. ALS, which invests in institutions focused on finding a cure and improving assistive technologies for ALS patients. Ed is the Chairman of the Advisory Board of Answer ALS.

Rapp is also a member of the AbbVie and XOS board of directors and serves on the Strategic Development board for the University of Missouri Business School. With his son, Rapp is involved in residential and commercial development and started Rapp Ventures, a private equity company focused on early-stage companies across a range of industries. Rapp also published *Measure Twice, Cut Once*, covering lessons learned throughout his career, and engages in discussions on the importance of work-life balance (https://youtu.be/Cd92mKdDE_c) and leading through adverse conditions.

Rapp has a BSBA degree in finance from the University of Missouri-Columbia and is a graduate of the University of Illinois Executive Development Program. Rapp and his wife, Ann, reside in Cary, North Carolina, near their children and grandsons.

Anju Jain is a business leader who has worked across multinational organizations in the U.S. and Asia. The bulk of her career was with Caterpillar Inc. in a variety of cross-functional roles, including Marketing, Finance, and HR. She was the Country HR Manager for India and ASEAN before she left Caterpillar to pursue book writing. She is an author of two books:

Burnout: *Beat Fatigue to Thrive in an Overworked World* (Penguin Random House, 2019)

Step Up: *How Women Can Perform Better for Success* (Penguin Random House, 2016)

Currently, Anju is the CHRO at Fermilab, America's particle physics and accelerator laboratory in Illinois. She holds a PhD in human development from Pennsylvania State University and lives with her family in Naperville, Illinois.

Printed in the USA
CPSIA information can be obtained
at www.ICGtesting.com
LVHW060819260524
780466LV00025B/168/J